THE ELEMENTS OF PROPHECY

R. J. Stewart is a Scottish author and composer who has worked, researched and written extensively on the western esoteric tradition. He has composed and recorded music for television, film, and stage and is the designer and player of the 80 stringed concert psaltery.

The *Elements of* is a series designed to present high quality introductions to a broad range of essential subjects.

The books are commissioned specifically from experts in their fields. They provide readable and often unique views of the various topics covered, and are therefore of interest both to those who have some knowledge of the subject, as well as those who are approaching it for the first time.

Many of these concise yet comprehensive books have practical suggestions and exercises which allow personal experience as well as theoretical understanding, and offer a valuable source of information on many important themes.

In the same series

THE ELEMENTS OF
PROPHECY

R J Stewart

ELEMENT BOOKS

First published in Great Britain in 1990 by
Element Books Limited
Longmead, Shaftesbury, Dorset

Designed by Jenny Liddle
Cover design by Max Fairbrother
Cover Illustration by Martin Rieser
Typeset by Selectmove Ltd, London

Printed and bound in Great Britain by
Billings, Hylton Road, Worcester

British Library Cataloguing in Publication Data
Stewart, R. J.
The elements of prophecy.
1. Prophecy
I. Title
133.3

ISBN 1–85230–134–1

CONTENTS

Appendices

FOREWORD

This book aims to show, in a short space, some of the basic elements of prophecy. The subject is immense, and there is no suggestion here, within the limited space available, that the more complex textual and cultural ramifications have been fully examined. It would take a very large book or set of volumes indeed to analyse and begin to interpret those intriguing interconnections between actual prophetic texts and methods in varying cultures and in different eras.

Why, for example, does a medieval text, *The Prophecies of Merlin*, contain elements of what seems to be ancient Greek astrology embedded within Celtic bardic tradition, when the astrology of the contemporary period was more likely to be Arabic? Why was prophecy distinctly frowned upon by political Christianity, yet prophetic texts and utterances, loosely disguised under a more or less orthodox framework, abounded even in the most repressive periods of Christian history. The famous prophet Michel de Notre Dame, Nostradamus (sixteenth century) openly describes his techniques of altered consciousness in a preface written to his infant son, yet modern attention is placed solely upon interpreting his obscure verses, rather than upon this important description of prophetic art, which is quoted in translation on pp.86–92. Nostradamus' *Preface à Mon Fils* has nothing Christian in it other than a few devout assertions of the supremacy of God, and, despite his Jewish origins, nothing similar to the very distinctive nature of Jewish prophecy, which is discussed in our later chapters in the Biblical Hebrew orthodox, and Kabbalistic contexts.

Indeed, Nostradamus was clearly of the same school as Merlin, whoever Merlin might have been,[1] perhaps representing an underground tradition of prophecy that persisted in attenuated but active forms from the ancient Greek and Celtic eras. We could continue with such fascinating questions for many hundreds of pages of comparison and interpretation: how much was the important text of the Book of Revelation in the Christian New Testament influenced by certain Jewish apocalyptic texts which were later excluded from the orthodox canons of both Judaism and Christianity? What connection, if any, does the Holy Quran have with earlier prophetic books? And if we have any doubt at all about effect or potency of prophecy in the present era, we need only to consider Islam, a way of life and religion founded solely upon inspired prophecy.

The interconnections – in any religion or other source, regardless of dogma – are, in my opinion, more representative of inherent qualities or properties of human consciousness than of historical or textual transfers through the media of trade, migration, literature and travelling entertainers or storytellers, or even of the major medium of religious dissemination. All of these undoubtedly occur in abundance, but the fundamentals of myth-making and prophecy remain the same, for they are the human response to the mysteries of the environment . . . an environment that begins with the locality and land, but ultimately extends to the stars.

The main thesis of this book is that prophecy is inextricably linked to Creation Myth:[2] both tell the story of the universe, the world, its inhabitants, the supernatural powers and divinities, and eventually of the end of a universal cycle.

It is difficult, though not impossible, to separate prophecy, divination, prediction, and other aspects of altered consciousness. It is equally difficult to distinguish between prophetic, religious, meditational and magical techniques: they all share many elements in common. As a general rule I have not made rigid distinctions, but have simply allowed the book to flow, rather than involve the reader in repetitious cross references and rigid definitions (such as 'for a definition of prophecy, see . . .' or 'for the difference between prophecy and divination, see . . .').

There are, however several interconnected definitions of prophecy, its relationship to divinatory arts, and the distinction between true prophecy and various kinds and levels of prediction offered in the chapters which follow. We might summarise these briefly here as three levels or spirals of consciousness (setting aside for the moment the argument regarding validity or accuracy):

1. prophecy
2. prediction or divination
3. forecasting

This relationship and its various subsets in actual prophetic or divinatory practices are discussed throughout the remainder of the book, with various examples drawn from sources ranging from ancient Assyria to twentieth-century Europe and America. I trust that the reader will be patient when the boundaries between these categories become blurred, as they often do, but the elaboration and discussion in the various chapters and the information and examples included from actual prophetic texts and methods will help to clarify in theory that which is often turbulent and paradoxical in practice.

A number of mythic cycles and formal religious texts preserve stories concerning the beginning and ending of the world; sometimes they refer to previous world orders that have been destroyed and rebuilt in a new form. The presence of chaotic imagery in prophecy often derives from such tales, using their vocabulary and symbols in a manner that represents the altered or heightened consciousness and the vision of the seer or seeress. But in addition to such a traditional mythic or religious vocabulary, prophets sometimes attempt to describe what they perceive in startling imagery, speaking of it in its own right, and seeking to reveal the vision, the entities and the forces, in dramatic and graphic terms that will galvanise the listener or reader into some new level or perception.

So we also have a number of highly individual texts preserved from various sources in which we find orthodox imagery and terminology fused with highly unorthodox visions.

In some prophetic or divinatory texts, however, we find quite the opposite concept, for the esoteric heart of the prophecy is deliberately hidden in obscure terminology, often requiring oral instruction or specific initiation into the school of symbolism within which the prophet originally trained. Some seers, particularly during the Christian era, couched their visions in very carefully worded and disguised language, for fear of reprisal. There are long literary traditions of Hermetic philosophy, Kabbala (though this is essentially an oral teaching), Alchemy, and Magical Arts, all of which contain prophetic or inspired lore disguised in complex symbolism and difficult language.

The modern commentator or reader, therefore, has the difficult task of deciding which aspects of a prophecy are traditional, mythic, and religious; which aspects are original and represent individual visions communicating higher consciousness; and which parts are cipher, double-blind, or secret message. And, of course, which texts are political propaganda (a major feature of many literary prophecies), mere nonsense, or blatant fraud.

Such are the elements of prophecy, and no one can truthfully claim to be able to untangle them, not even a prophet.

PREDESTINATION?

One of the repeated questions which arises in the context of divination or prophecy is that of predestination. If Merlin, Ezekiel, Moses, Nostradamus or Edgar Cayce foretold that certain things would come to pass, if the Book of Revelation is true prophetic vision, what hope have we as individuals of transforming our lives, or our world, for the better? Are we not condemned to the collective fate, the terrible visions described by seers or sybils since the dawn of human culture?

The entire argument between free will and predestination occupied many thinkers and writers for centuries, and was sometimes a raging argument indeed. Had God predestined the end of the world or could humanity, through free will or perhaps the redemption of a Saviour, escape – or, better still, transform – that terrible fate? On a less exalted level, if your own life is shown in an astrological chart, does this not fix your patterns, and make your life a straitjacket? No modern astrologer would argue in favour of this theory, but it was firmly adhered to by many medieval and Renaissance astrologers. And what if a Tarot reading, carried out on the most simple level of daily prediction, shows terrible events or potential misery? Are we bound by this simplistic vision? Once we descend to this lowest level of divination, most people begin to resist and disavow, but the higher collective planetary visions of disaster are now an economic, political, and environmental reality.

Interestingly the entire formal discussion of the relationship between free will and predestination has virtually ceased today: perhaps nobody takes it seriously, or perhaps we have experienced the beginnings of a change in collective consciousness that will enable us to dispose of such rigid assumptions that these terms are irreconcilable opposites. While predestination was a feature of medieval astrology and religion, it does not seem to have played a great part in the operation of inherent or inspired prophecy. If we consider the

Old Testament prophets, they did indeed utter predictions, often of dire consequences, but this was always tempered by the message that if the Children of Israel returned to the ways of righteousness, then such evils might be averted. We now tend cynically to regard this as mere propaganda, but this concept of alternatives runs through many prophecies that are not part of a dogmatic or, as in the case of Christianity, a political, religion. Once prophecy extends into politics, then we find it used as propaganda and, curiously, we find the princes and politicians of the world seeking to enter prophecies, to enact within their own lives that which was predicted. No one is less secure than the powerful ruler. This aspect of prophecy in history is briefly discussed in Chapter 9.

The *Prophecies of Merlin*, for example, discussed in Chapters 5 and 8, make what appear to be a number of accurate predictions concerning the future, extending centuries ahead of their medieval period. But they also seem to reveal the means to avert the very disasters which they describe, for they contain a number of mystical and magical images and techniques. Most significant of all, they contain a strongly developed awareness of the sanctity of the land, something which we are only now, towards the close of the twentieth century, regaining. The *Centuries* (so called because there are one hundred verses to each volume) of Nostradamus seem to offer a number of prophecies that have come true, even down to specific dates, yet there are many verses that are incomprehensible. We could continue to cite examples at great length, and would always find this mixture of accuracy and apparent inaccuracy.

There are various rather complex and often tedious philosophical and metaphysical explanations for this variable factor in prophecy, and there is also, of course, the simple common-sense explanation that hindsight can explain anything as foresight. It seems likely, from the various descriptions made by seers, sybils and prophets, that the true prophetic consciousness transcends time, space, and events. Thus it perceives archetypical potentials, which may manifest in serial time and space, in several possible final forms. This is similar to the concept of infinite parallel realities used by modern philosophers and physicists.[3]

We should certainly dispose of the idea of a rigid predestination, for that leaves us open to manipulation and abuse by the dogma-mongers. Yet it is clear that perfect free will cannot exist, for life is a matter of interaction – all entities and energies interact with one another. The prophet, therefore, defines potentials, and describes how these potentials might appear in the outer or serial or manifest world. It is irrelevant whether prophecies are 'right' or 'wrong', but it is important that we consider the potentials described, particularly when we find them resonating to the rhythm of our own time and place, and relating to our own collective and individual choices and potentials.

INTRODUCTION:
WHAT IS PROPHECY?

Prophecy is itself a spiritual and psychic event that has influenced
the development of humankind upon the planet, and which forms,
as a secondary ramification of the prophetic event itself, one of the
foundations for cultures and religions through history.

Prophecy is a feature of human life, of human consciousness. It is
not idle superstition, unhealthy longing after the forbidden future, or
the sole property of patriarchs ruling dogmatic religions. If you think
that prophecy is part of the outmoded unscientific superstitious past,
then consider the Stock Exchange, or consider the vast computers
dedicated to military strategy or to weather forecasting. None of
these modern phenomena is truly prophetic in itself, but they clearly
indicate our deep involvement in seeking the pattern of events, even
to the extent of vast technological investment for fairly inaccurate
returns.

Most of this pursuit is frantic, seeking a totally false security
in 'knowing the future' for purely selfish, even dangerous, ends:
here is the crucial difference between prophecy, prediction, and
forecasting, to which we shall return in more detail shortly. For the
moment we might consider that pure prophecy is selfless, prediction
is potentially unbiased but often moulded or falsified in practice,
whereas forecasting is usually undertaken solely for self-interest.
But beyond the trivial level, there is an inherent drive within us to
grasp, to perceive, patterns beyond those of regular habit, beyond

apparent 'cause and effect'. The selfish wish to know the future is merely the lowest level of this inherent projection of consciousness beyond serial time and events.

Such patterns or insights as are found in true prophecy are frequently called transcendent in modern literature, but this tends to reinforce our unfortunate linear mode of thought, suggesting that they are 'above' us, or 'superior', when in fact they are present in everyday life. Prophetic and esoteric traditions offer a number of models that help us to grasp this situation, but at this stage it is enough to suggest that while the 'higher' modes of perception or rates of consciousness are indeed inherent and present in immediate daily life, they are filtered through various mental and emotional states of colouration and interpretation.

The task of reaching these universal patterns or modes of consciousness is not so much one of leaving everyday patterns behind, but of transmuting them, of re-attuning them so that their filtering effect becomes helpful and clarifying, rather than obstructive and obscuring. Only at this stage may we liberate ourselves from the apparent sequence of cause and effect.

Paradoxically, computers, set up to crunch numbers into a resolution of sequences, to state the end products of seeming cause and effect, are now beginning to show that this causal premise is, in itself, inherently inaccurate, even untrue. This is no more than what the mystical or esoteric traditions have asserted for millennia, while offering their own stringent methods, disciplines and tests whereby individuals may validate or repudiate such assertions for themselves.

Recent developments in computer forecasting have shown that there are modes or patterns which are not susceptible to computer analysis, world weather being particularly 'existential'. Curiously, much of the ancient prophetic tradition is concerned with weather, not only in terms of daily life or annual harvest, but weather as a pattern, a holism concerned with the land, the planet, the stars. Little wonder, therefore, that our computers cannot always predict the weather with a degree of accuracy, for if the ancient traditions are correct the interaction of the entire planet, solar system, even the universe, would have to be contained and modelled within the data and programmes of the computer. Human consciousness, however, possesses certain abilities that enable it, albeit rarely, to apprehend such universal patterns: this is true prophecy.

8

THE THREE WORLDS: A HARMONIC MODEL

For practical purposes we may use a simple threefold spiral or pattern of concentric circles, often known as The Three Worlds, to give us a framework within which to examine prophecy. The word 'framework' is perhaps misleading, for it suggests something rigid, with hard boundaries and levels: there are no such firm boundaries in human awareness, or indeed in the universe itself. The triple pattern is really something *harmonic*, pertaining more to the realm of music than to mechanics: each level or spiral is a harmonic sequence of over-tones, an interpenetrating set of relationships. Thus the Three Worlds (see Figure 1) are three coexisting modes of perception, or rates of consciousness: we may limit our understanding of them to this interpretation, though it is only proper to state that in the prophetic traditions themselves the worlds – three, seven, nine, twelve, or innumerable – are also regarded as dimensions or planes of existence in their own right.

These other worlds have inhabitants, and may be accessed by humanity; ... likewise the otherworlds may reach directly into our world. The ultimate prophetic consciousness is when spiritual or divine Being utters truth through a human vehicle.

The octave – by which we recognise the same note at twice the rate, a high and low note, but nevertheless the same note – is perhaps the most clear example of energetic or musical proportions. The law of octaves applies directly to consciousness – indeed according to the ancient philosophers and metaphysicians, the universe is music.[4] As much of our historical evidence of prophecy comes from cultures in which this holistic attitude was inherent, we need to have a simple modern model of such a holism, rather than attempt to force prophetic traditions and events into a pseudo-rationalistic interpretation or, worse, some kind of pseudo-scientific justification.

Prophecy is itself a spiritual and psychic event that has influenced the development of humankind upon the planet, and which forms, as a secondary ramification of the event itself, the foundation for cultures and religions through history.

The triple spiral of Figure 1 defines three levels or harmonics: prophecy, prediction, forecasting. These correspond to the traditional Three Worlds and to modes of consciousness as follows:

1. prophecy—Spirit; universal consciousness; Stellar World
2. prediction—Soul; integrated or harmonic consciousness; Solar World

9

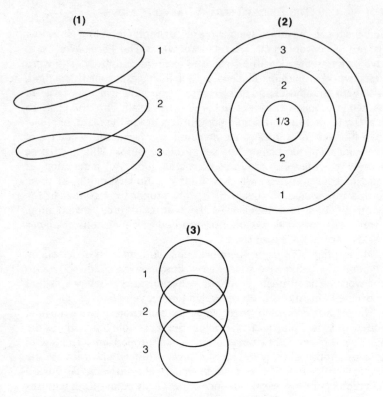

Figure 1   The Three Worlds

1. Supernal or prophetic consciousness (Stellar Universe)
2. Transpersonal or spiritual consciousness (Solar System)
3. Personal or psychic consciousness (Lunar and Earth World)

3. forecasting—Mind/emotions; regular interacting consciousness,
    including the unconscious mind; Lunar World

Each spiral or octave of consciousness manifests in the outer,
everyday, material, collective world of human life upon the planet
Earth. They tend to flow through one another, and although most of
us can forecast either by deduction, built up by the complex structure
of memory from direct life experience (excluding for the moment
advanced methods of deduction or computers), or by intuition, and

many of us may accurately predict events through an indefinable inner certainty (excluding, for the moment, the use of specialised techniques and devices for prediction), very few of us experience the flash of direct prophetic inspiration.

The three harmonics of prophetic consciousness may broadly correspond to three typical inner experiences within the individual, though there is no hard and fast rule other than the triple harmonic sequence itself:

1. Insight is a harmonic of Prophecy
2. Farsight is a harmonic of Prediction
3. Divination is a harmonic of Foresight[5]

These harmonics are found through inner realisation, or in meditation, and may also appear suddenly as moments of personal or transpersonal revelation. Many of the ancient techniques for expanding consciousness begin with divinatory methods designed to lead to deeper and more valuable levels of awareness, such as farsight (in which perception reaches beyond the individual limited circle of attention), and insight (in which a similar threshold is crossed inwardly, reaching to levels of consciousness or realms of inner being that have hitherto been closed to the individual).

PROPHETIC MESSAGES AND UTTERANCES

A number of typical modes of prophecy prediction or divination have existed from the earliest history.

1. The mode which should be considered as true prophecy is that in which the consciousness is transformed and inspired, so that the prophet or seer is impelled to utter truth. This movement of humanity by divine or transcendent consciousness or beings – such as gods or goddesses and also in the classical world daemones or heroes – works through the three levels of the Three Worlds. Direct revelation and inspiration are the highest and rarest level of this mode of prophetic knowledge. At the lower harmonics we find images arising in the consciousness, fragments of communication and conceptual implications, and simple factual knowledge. These aspects, communicated both through waking states and in dreams, or in specially induced trances and sleep states, merge with the arts of divination and practical forecasting. Many of the divinations of the ancient world were very simple and mundane.

2. The second mode is that of holistic resonance, frequently debased as crude animistic augury or rule-of-thumb tables of correspondences. This includes divination through animal sacrifice and the study of organs (see also pp.32–34), the movement of animals and birds, and the paradoxical presence of divinity in simple objects, suddenly invested with potency and articulate with prophetic meaning. The systems of augury known in the ancient world, and perpetuated to the present day in folklore, represent, at their best level, examples of holistic resonance, in which the human awareness suddenly knows of future or distant events by observing something close and simple and (superficially) unrelated. The investment or charging of a simple object with divine energy or consciousness is clearly related to this, but on a higher level of the spiral of harmonic consciousness. Examples of this include the famous incident of the Burning Bush in the Old Testament (though our third mode, shortly to be described, may also be included) and the well-attested mystical inspirational state in which everyday objects are discovered to be filled with glory, divinity and transcendent Being, sometimes speaking through explicit images or sudden transformations of trees, stones, or other natural phenomena.

3. The third mode is that of the direct voice from the otherworld or from divinity, a voice heard literally with the ears, and not an inner intimation or subtle whisper. This was well known to the ancient Hebrews, and many of the Semitic prophetic utterances or texts are said to have originated in this manner, by voices directly speaking to the prophet or even to an assembled gathering. In Genesis xxii, the Angel of the Lord calls out to Abraham to save Isaac whom he is about to sacrifice. In the New Testament a voice speaks directly to Saul, apparently that of Jesus, asking him why he continues to persecute the prophet's followers. Other voices are heard in the New Testament, at the baptism of Jesus by John, and in John xii, where some hear the voice of an angel speaking, while others in the crowd hear thunder. A voice is heard again by the assembled followers at the Transfiguration of Jesus.

The direct voice from heaven, though frequently popularised in fantasy films involving Greek gods, did not play a major part in Greek tradition. The gods did, however, have the disconcerting habit of appearing in physical form and talking man to man. Epiphanies, or highly potent and significant symbolic appearances of gods and goddesses, often occurred at sacred temple sites, or at locations where a temple should be built. But when we turn to Roman mythology –

and, indeed, to recorded Roman history – we find that the prophetic voice of divinity reappears as an accepted feature of communication and prediction. In Cicero's *De Divinatione*, a book which we shall cite further in later chapters, we find:

> Often have Fauns been heard speaking in battles, and in times of trouble voices are said to come forth from the unseen and to have been proved true. Out of a great multitude of such cases, let me give two signal ones. Just before the City (of Rome) was captured by the Gauls, a voice was heard issuing from the grove of Vesta, ordering that the walls and gates be repaired ... unless that were done in time Rome would fall. This warning was disregarded, though the great catastrophe might still have been prevented; atonement was made after the event; an altar was dedicated on the spot (where the voice was heard) to *Aius Loquens* [the Speaker]. Again, many writers have recorded that when the earthquake happened, a voice issued from the temple of Juno in the citadel, commanding the sacrifice of a pregnant sow as a means of aversion. For this reason Juno was called *Moneta* [Warning].

In these two Roman examples we find a typical fusion of prophetic utterance, myth, and an underlying tone of magical arts from deep layers of chthonic religion, for in both cases the voices are uttered from significant locations, the grove of the Virgin goddess Vesta, and, in the case of Juno, demanding the sacrifice of a pregnant sow, the beast dedicated to the Dark Goddess of the Underworld, Hecate. The implications and cross references of such utterances, both the Hebrew and Roman, are typical of many such examples and would not have been lost on contemporary people, for they were interwoven within the mythic structure of the religion of the times and place.

In mystical experience, the exterior voice, found in mythology and religion, becomes inseparable from the interior voice. Many inspirations, examples of prophetic knowledge, and simple utterance of personal insight or spiritual truth, seem to come as voices speaking directly into the ear of the seer or mystic or magician. We should, however, exercise considerable caution with regard to such experiences, and especially when such voices are heard in personal meditation. The best judgement is common sense, for if the *audition*, as it is often called, is trivial gossip, nonsense or random words, then it is clearly valueless.

13

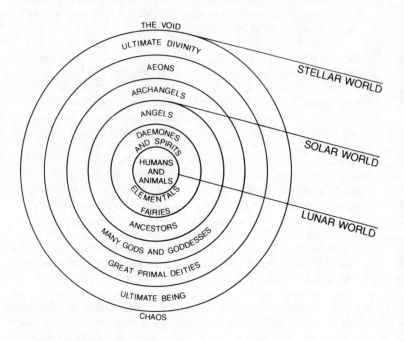

Figure 2   Sources of prophetic inspiration in the Three Worlds

In the classical world the communications of *daimones*, a type of spirit living between the Earth and the Moon (see Figure 2) were often experienced. Though this type of entity was much later rationalised and propagandised into the Christian demon, the original concept was not one of evil or temptation.

The philosopher Socrates was sometimes visited by a *daimonion* – the word strictly implies a neuter form of *daimonios*, 'a divine something'. In much later times we find that the prophet Merlin was the offspring of a *daimon* and a human mother, and in the *Vita Merlini* the old classical Creation myth was reworked and fused with Celtic tradition, by which the *daimones* are spirits, yet close enough to humanity to breed with mortal women. Even in the Merlin texts there is no strong suggestion that Merlin's father was an evil demon,

14

though this type of propaganda was to develop later, when the political Church felt obliged to repress native prophecies and ancient legends. In the case of Socrates, his guiding entity would suddenly impress certain knowledge or inhibitions upon him, coming, as it were, from another dimension.

In Rabbinical texts we find something called the Daughter of the Voice, the *bath-qol*. This was regarded as a harmonic or reflection of the actual Voice of God, and it is interesting that its gender was female, for this is typical of the laws of polarity inherent in many mystical and metaphysical teachings, including the Kabbalah. 'The voice which came forth from heaven was not itself heard, but from his voice proceeded another voice, just as when a man strikes an object with force you may hear a second sound in the distance proceeding from the first sound.' The *bath-qol* was heard by assembled rabbis and mystics, and many examples are recorded. It often gave indications of holiness, or of textual interpretations, and seems to have been, at times, a collective spiritual insight due to prayer and meditation. In Josephus, and in Rabbinical tradition, we find the story of the High Priest John Hyrcanus (135–104 BC), who heard a voice (*bath-qol*) issuing from the Holy of Holies proclaiming victory for the Jewish army at Antioch. On the death of Moses, the Daughter of the Voice was heard throughout the camp of Israel. Ultimately, however the *bath-qol* was regarded, by the Hebrews, as a lesser and possibly even an undesirable effect. What the Hebrew prophets required, and often obtained, was the direct voice of God, nothing less.

As in many of the examples of prophetic utterance that we might cite, we should remind ourselves that we set aside, for the present, the discussion that has persisted since classical times, or perhaps earlier, concerning the validity of certain utterances and the frivolity or insanity of others. Many people seem to hear voices which are trivial, depraved, absurd, or simply distracting and irrelevant. Clearly these cannot all be prophetic or otherworldly, and many are simply the results of mental imbalance. This discussion, between the merits of prophetic utterance and the possibilities of madness, will be touched upon in various places in this book, but is nowadays the property of psychology rather than of philosophy or mysticism. The psychologist dares to judge the individual, but the individual philosopher, seer or mystic must ultimately judge for himself or herself.

4. A fourth mode is that of the written communication from the otherworld or from divinity. This is an enduring concept, and many examples could be cited from the most ancient times to the present

day. In Chapter 33 of the *Egyptian Book of the Dead* we find the following remarkable passage:

> This chapter was found in the city of Hemmennu under the feet of this god. It was inscribed upon a slab of iron of the south, in the writing of the god himself, in the time of the majesty of the king Men-kau-Ra, by the royal son Heru-ta-ta-f, who discovered it whilst he was on his journey to make an inspection of the temples and their estates

[trans. Wallis-Budge].

The cynical among us will consider it not impossible that a member of the priestly aristocracy might forge such an inscription for his own ends, but it seems certain that the ancients believed implicitly in the reality of such divine messages.

In the Old Testament there is the famous example of the two tables of the Law, written upon stone by the finger of God, though Moses copied the original divine inscription. In Ezekiel we find the concept of a written message from God, but perceived in a vision: 'when I looked, behold, a hand was put forth unto me, and lo a roll of a book was written within and without, and there was written therein lamentation and mourning and woe' (Ezekiel ii: 9). In Zechariah we find another such vision, one which was to have an influence, along with many other such prophetic but physical messages, upon a much later semi-religious movement in the nineteenth and early twentieth centuries.

> I lifted up my eyes and, behold, a flying roll. And he said unto me, What seest thou? And I answered a flying roll, the length thereof is twenty cubits and the breadth thereof ten cubits. Then he said unto me, This is the curse that goeth forth over the face of the whole land. I will cause it to go forth, saith the Lord of Hosts, and it shall enter into the house of the thief, and into the house of him that sweareth falsely by My Name, and it shall abide in the midst of his house, and shall consume it . . .

[Zechariah v: 1]

Zechariah also gives further visions in the same chapter, including a typical prophetic and perhaps apocalyptic vision of different coloured horses drawing chariots to each of Four Quarters. We shall return to the words 'flying roll' shortly.

In classical sources we find that Askelpios (Asculapius) the god of therapy, son of Apollo, delivered written messages to supplicants. Pausanius, in the second century AD cites a story involving a historical person, an Arcadian poetess, Anyte, some of whose work is still preserved today. When she slept in the temple of Askelpios at Epidaurus, she dreamed that a tablet (inscribed with a message but sealed) was in her hand. On awakening she found that such a message was indeed in her hand, and followed the bidding of the god, which was to lead to a miraculous cure for blindness for the recipient of the sealed tablet.

In the third century AD a Syrian called Alcibiades brought a sacred book to Rome: this, he claimed, had been delivered from heaven by an enormous angel. It became the sacred text of the Christian sect of the Elkasaites, who claimed that it had been given to them by the Chinese, or rather to their founder Elchasai. The Elkasaites seem to have been a short-lived movement, with the sacred book being based upon fairly standard Judaeo-Christian precepts.

We find a similar tale told by Joseph Smith, founder of the substantial sect of the Mormons, a branch of Christianity now found worldwide. He claimed to have found the *Book of Mormon* engraved upon gold plates, in the USA. An angel had revealed their hiding place to him on 21 September 1823. (As an interesting aside, which I cannot vouch for personally nor support, a student of Hebrew once told me that the words Mormon and Moroni, which are central to this sect, seem to mean 'a fraud for the purpose of obtaining money'.) Not long after this we find the Theosophical Society, based in London, but with a far-reaching influence as it grew, receiving Flying Rolls. These were physical letters manifesting suddenly from hidden Masters, sent to guide their pupils in the way of wisdom.

The term Flying Roll was also used to describe documents by the Hermetic Order of the Golden Dawn, one of the most famous magical orders, which still has active temples operating to this day. Indeed, in magical orders, the tradition of physical messages manifesting is strangely persistent, though it is often modified to the other traditional practice connected to such messages, which is that they are dictated by an innerworld or divine source, but written out by the seer or adept. One of the more famous examples of such a text is Aliester Crowley's *Book of the Law*, dictated to him in Egypt by an otherworldly being, and at first rejected by him until he was later compelled to accept its validity. Another such example is the complex and slightly stuffy cosmological text *The Cosmic Doctrine*, dictated to the occultist Dion Fortune by an innerworld Master. Once again, we can only judge such material

17

by its actual content, and not prejudge it by the story surrounding its manifestation.

In European Christianity, particularly in Germany, there is an enduring belief in a specific letter from Heaven, which is said to have fallen to Earth at Jerusalem or Rome, and to have been written by Christ, God, or perhaps the Archangel Michael. The original letter disappeared, it is said, but a holy man made a copy of it before it vanished, and copies of this copy were circulated and eventually printed. This story originated at least as early as the sixth century AD, when Bishop Vincentius read the letter from Heaven (*Himmelsbrief*) to a congregation in the Balearic Islands, telling that it had been written by Christ and delivered by falling from Heaven on to the altar of St Peter.

Versions reappeared continually through the Middle Ages: by the year 1260, some six hundred years or more after its first appearance in Europe, people were expecting the end of the world. Indeed, the end had been prophesied by Joachim of Fiore (see Chapter 9), and there was a general surge of apocalyptic fervour and penitence. The active sect of Flagellants, who whipped and scourged themselves from place to place, sang a version of the Letter as a type of anthem or hymn.

By the fifteenth century we find that a versified version of the Letter was written out (the manuscript is still preserved in the Bodleian Library). Soon it was to pass into print and remain in various versions into the twentieth century, mainly in Germany, including versions printed for soldiers during the First and Second World Wars. Such is the continuity of belief in the manifestation of written utterance from Heaven, merging with cynical propaganda.

Clearly some of the examples listed above hardly merit the term prophecy, for they are on that confused borderline between prophecy, myth, and superstition. While we might exclude, for example, all stories of written messages and manifesting prophecies, to do so would be to omit a range of human experience and belief concerning such matters than runs actively from ancient Egypt to modern Europe.

To conclude this Introduction, we may briefly consider some extracts from the detailed analysis of prophecy made by Thomas Aquinas in his *Summa Theologica*: in these instances, of course, the approach is a precise analysis from the viewpoint of Christian dogma, but the inherent source material, drawn from the vast inheritance of the classical world, is of great value.

Now all prophecy is according to the Divine foreknowledge, since the prophets *read in the book of foreknowledge*, as a gloss says on

Isa. xxxviii. 1. Therefore it would seem that prophecy according to foreknowledge should not be reckoned a species of prophecy.

Obj. 2. Further, Just as something is foretold in denunciation, so is something foretold in promise, and both of these are subject to alteration. For it is written (Jer. xviii. 7, 8): *I will suddenly speak against a nation and against a kingdom, to root out, and to pull down, and to destroy it. If that nation against which I have spoken shall repent of their evil, I also will repent – and* this pertains to the prophecy of denunciation, and afterwards the text continues in reference to the prophecy of promise (*verses* 9, 10): *I will suddenly speak of a nation and of a kingdom, to build up and plant it. If it shall do evil in My sight . . . I will repent of the good that I have spoken to do unto it.* Therefore as there is reckoned to be a prophecy of denunciation, so should there be a prophecy of promise.

Obj. 3. Further, Isidore says (*Etym.* vii. 8): *There are seven kinds of prophecy. The first is an ecstasy, which is the transport of the mind:* thus Peter saw a vessel descending from heaven with all manner of beasts therein. *The second kind is a vision, as we read in Isaias, who says* (vi. 1): 'I saw the Lord sitting,' etc. *The third kind is a dream:* thus Jacob in a dream, saw a ladder. *The fourth kind is from the midst of a cloud:* thus God spake to Moses. *The fifth kind is* a voice from heaven, *as that which called to Abraham saying* (Gen. xxii. 2): 'Lay not thy hand upon the boy.' *The sixth kind is* taking up a parable, *as in the example of Balaam* (Num. xxiii. 7, xxiv. 15). *The seventh kind is the fulness of the Holy Ghost, as in the case of nearly all the prophets.* Further, he mentions three kinds of vision; one by the eyes of the body, another by the soul's imagination, a third by the eyes of the mind. Now these are not included in the aforesaid division. Therefore it is insufficient.

On the contrary stands the authority of Jerome to whom the gloss above quoted is ascribed.

I answer that, The species of moral habits and acts are distinguished according to their objects. Now the object of prophecy is something known by God and surpassing the faculty of man. Wherefore, according to the difference of such things, prophecy is divided into various species, as assigned above. Now it has been stated above (Q. LXXI., A. 6, *ad* 2) that the future is contained in the Divine knowledge in two ways. First, as in its cause: and thus we have the prophecy of denunciation, which is not always fulfilled; but it foretells the relation of cause to effect, which is sometimes hindered by some other occurrence supervening. Secondly, God foreknows certain things in themselves, – either as to be accomplished by Himself, and of such things is the prophecy of *predestination*, since, according to Damascene (*De Fide Orthod*. ii. 30), *God predestines things which are not in our power*, – or as to be accomplished through man's free-will, and of such is the prophecy of *foreknowledge*. This may regard either good or evil, which does not apply to the prophecy of predestination, since the latter regards good alone. And since predestination is comprised under foreknowledge, the gloss in the beginning of the Psalter assigns only two species to prophecy, namely of *foreknowledge*, and of *denunciation*.

Reply Obj. 1. Foreknowledge, properly speaking, denotes precognition of future events in themselves, and in this sense it is reckoned a species of prophecy. But in so far as it is used in connexion with future events, whether as in themselves, or as in their causes, it is common to every species of prophecy.

Reply Obj. 2. The prophecy of promise is included in the prophecy of denunciation, because the aspect of truth is the same in both. But it is denominated in preference from denunciation, because God is more inclined to remit punishment than to withdraw promised blessings.

Reply Obj. 3. Isidore divides prophecy according to the manner of prophesying. Now we may distinguish the manner of prophesying, – either according to man's cognitive powers, which are sense, imagination, and intellect, and then we have the three kinds of vision mentioned both by him and by Augustine (*Gen. ad Lit*. xii. 6, 7), – or according to the different ways in which the prophetic current is received. Thus as regards the enlightening of the intellect there is the *fulness of the Holy Ghost* which he mentions in the seventh place. As to the imprinting of pictures on the imagination he mentions three, namely *dreams*, to which he gives the third place; *vision*, which occurs to the prophet while awake and regards any kind of ordinary object, and this he puts in the second place; and *ecstasy*, which results from the mind being uplifted to certain lofty things, and to this he assigns the first place. As regards sensible signs he reckons three kinds of prophecy, because a sensible sign is, – either a corporeal thing offered externally to the sight, such as *a cloud*, which he mentions in the fourth place, – or a *voice* sounding from without and conveyed to man's hearing, – this he puts in the fifth place, – or a voice proceeding from a man, conveying something under a similitude, and this pertains to the *parable* to which he assigns the sixth place.

WHETHER THE PROPHECY WHICH IS ACCOMPANIED BY INTELLECTIVE
AND IMAGINATIVE VISION IS MORE EXCELLENT THAN THAT WHICH IS
ACCOMPANIED BY INTELLECTIVE VISION ALONE?

We proceed thus to the Second Article:

Objection 1. It would seem that the prophecy which has intellective and imaginative vision is more excellent than that which is accompanied by intellective vision alone. For Augustine says (*Gen. ad Lit.* xii. 9): *He is less a prophet, who sees in spirit nothing but the signs representative of things, by means of the images of things corporeal: he is more a prophet, who is merely endowed with the understanding of these signs; but most of all is he a prophet, who excels in both ways,* and this refers to the prophet who has intellective together with imaginative vision. Therefore this kind of prophecy is more excellent.

Obj. 2. Further, The greater a thing's power is, the greater the distance to which it extends. Now the prophetic light pertains chiefly to the mind, as stated above (Q. CLXXIII., A. 2). Therefore apparently the prophecy that extends to the imagination is greater than that which is confined to the intellect.

Obj. 3. Further, Jerome (*Prol. in Lib. Reg.*) distinguishes the *prophets* from the *sacred writers*. Now all those whom he calls prophets (such as Isaias, Jeremias, and the like) had intellective together with imaginative vision: but not those whom he calls sacred writers, as writing by the inspiration of the Holy Ghost (such as Job, David, Solomon, and the like). Therefore it would seem more proper to call prophets those who had intellective together with imaginative vision, than those who had intellective vision alone.

Obj. 4. Further, Dionysius says (*Cœl. Hier.* i.) that *it is impossible for the Divine ray to shine on us, except as screened round about by the many-coloured sacred veils.* Now the prophetic revelation is conveyed by the infusion of the divine ray. Therefore it seems that it cannot be without the veils of phantasms.

On the contrary, A gloss says at the beginning of the Psalter that *the most excellent manner of prophecy is when a man prophesies by the mere inspiration of the Holy Ghost, apart from any outward assistance of deed, word, vision, or dream.*

I answer that, The excellence of the means is measured chiefly by the end. Now the end of prophecy is the manifestation of a truth that surpasses the faculty of man. Wherefore the more effective this manifestation is, the more excellent the prophecy. But it is evident that the manifestation of divine truth by means of the bare contemplation of the truth itself, is more effective than that which is conveyed under the similitude of corporeal things, for it approaches nearer to the heavenly vision whereby the truth is seen in God's essence. Hence it follows that the prophecy whereby a supernatural truth is seen by intellectual vision, is more excellent than that in which a supernatural truth is manifested by means of the similitudes of corporeal things in the vision of the imagination.

Moreover the prophet's mind is shown thereby to be more lofty: even as in human teaching the hearer, who is able to grasp the bare intelligible truth the master propounds, is shown to have a better understanding than one who needs to be taken by the hand and helped by means of examples taken from objects of sense. Hence it is said in commendation of David's prophecy (2 Kings xxiii. 3): *The strong one of Israel spoke* to me, and further on (verse 4): *As the light of the morning, when the sun riseth, shineth in the morning without clouds.*

Reply Obj. 1. When a particular supernatural truth has to be revealed by means of corporeal images, he that has both, namely the intellectual light and the imaginary vision, is more a prophet than he that has only one, because his prophecy is more perfect; and it is in this sense that Augustine speaks as quoted above. Nevertheless the prophecy in which the bare intelligible truth is revealed is greater than all.

Reply Obj. 2. The same judgement does not apply to things that are sought for their own sake, as to things sought for the sake of something else. For in things sought for their own sake, the agent's power is the more effective according as it extends to more numerous and more remote objects; even so a physician is thought more of, if he is able to heal more people, and those who are further removed from health. On the other hand, in things sought only for the sake of something else, that agent would seem to have greater power, who is able to achieve his purpose with fewer means and those nearest to hand: thus more praise is awarded the physician who is able to heal a sick person by means of fewer and more gentle remedies. Now, in the prophetic knowledge, imaginary vision is required, not for its own sake, but on account of the manifestation of the intelligible truth. Wherefore prophecy is all the more excellent according as it needs it less.

Reply Obj. 3. The fact that a particular predicate is applicable to one thing and less properly to another, does not prevent this latter from being simply better than the former: thus the knowledge of the blessed is more excellent than the knowledge of the wayfarer, although faith is more properly predicated of the latter knowledge, because faith implies an imperfection of knowledge. In like manner prophecy implies a certain obscurity, and remoteness from the intelligible truth; wherefore the name of prophet is more properly applied to those who see by imaginary vision. And yet the more excellent prophecy is that which is conveyed by intellectual vision, provided the same truth be revealed in either case. If, however, the intellectual light be divinely infused in a person, not that he may know some supernatural things, but that he may be able to judge, with the certitude of divine truth, of things that can be known by human reason, such intellectual prophecy is beneath that which is conveyed by an imaginary vision leading to a supernatural truth. It was this kind of prophecy that all those had who are included in the ranks of the prophets, who moreover were called prophets for the special reason that they exercised the prophetic calling officially. Hence they spoke as God's representatives, saying to the people: *Thus saith the Lord*: but not so the authors of the 'sacred writings,' several of whom treated more frequently of things that can be known by human reason, not in God's name, but in their own, yet with the assistance of the Divine light withal.

Reply Obj. 4. In the present life the enlightenment by the divine ray is not altogether without any veil of phantasms, because according to his present state of life it is unnatural to man not to understand without a phantasm. Sometimes, however, it is sufficient to have phantasms abstracted in the usual way from the senses without any imaginary vision divinely vouchsafed, and thus prophetic vision is said to be without imaginary vision.

(Thomas Aquinas, *Summa Theologica*, Q.174, articles 1 and 2)

1 · HISTORICAL PERSPECTIVES:
PROPHECY THEN AND NOW

There is no realistic history of prophecy: by its very nature it defies normal historical concepts and is not bound by the artificial strictures of serial time. Even if we set aside the discussion of prophecy as a true ability and consider only historical evidence without attempting to validate or invalidate prophecy itself, there is still no historical progression to be defined. Prophecy is not, like certain other skills such as those of cultural development, traceable in an apparently linear or progressive manner. It does not originate, develop, regress, or become transmitted through various cultures. Like all true properties of consciousness, it is protean and appears in various resonant or harmonically related forms in every phase of human society, regardless of the social conditions or the type of civilisation. We may, however, trace certain historical aspects of the art or disciplines of prophecy, those same arts that were to give rise to the materialist sciences of the present day through the routes of astrology leading to astronomy, alchemy and magical arts to chemistry and physics, and so forth.

It is commonly asserted that prophecy plays little or no part in modern materialist society, that it is outmoded superstition. This is, of course, nonsense, for a major part of the material progress of our culture has been towards ever more definable prediction, involving technology and statistics.

Science is now discovering, however, that there are orders of result, apparent conclusions, resolution of data, of patterns, that simply do not correspond or fit within the linear materialist viewpoint. These paradoxes, defined by modern physics in the main, are within the realms not only of consciousness, but of universal entity. Prophecy likewise deals with connectives that are usually unperceived within the holism of the universe. In biology a number of recent developments have occurred which appear to relate to the perennial esoteric traditions, though it would be unfair to suggest that the researchers and theorists concerned are necessarily conscious of or willing to accept such a relationship. In biology perhaps the most recent theory that seems to attune to esoteric tradition is that of morphic resonance[6] which is a reasoned modern restatement of the spiritual tradition of images, life-forms, energy and consciousness, as timeless forms or archetypes. Interestingly this theory, be it ancient or modern, is central to the potential of prophecy and accurate prediction.

Furthermore we tend to sneer at the superstition of ancient cultures, or indeed the more recent and credulous times of our ancestors, at least until the eighteenth or early nineteenth centuries. This strange and hypocritical attitude should be balanced by facing up to the remarkable upsurge of occult and superstitious lore in the late nineteenth and twentieth centuries. There was indeed a slight lull in overt superstition both within and without religion and occultism at the close of the eighteenth and early nineteenth centuries, but the majority of people have remained susceptible to predictive and prophetic lore in an unbroken stream from the earliest times to the present day.

There is a frequent tendency, deriving from simple ignorance, to confuse popular superstition, which is often of the most vacuous and trivial kind, with the very highly disciplined techniques and systems found within perennial wisdom teachings, religions, and spiritual arts and disciplines. Nor is this situation helped by the fact that perennial tradition is often preserved in folklore and mythic tales, songs, and customs, right alongside trivial superstition and debased magical practices. This last situation is, historically, the result of a culture or cultures being fragmented by an invading or oppressive state religion, such as has occurred with political Christianity. More simply, older orders remain as partly hidden traditions beneath whatever is imposed upon the collective consciousness by force or political decree. Much of the deep-rooted acceptance of or longing for prophecy and related inner perceptions is rooted at this hidden level, but frequently breaks through into everyday life as popular, trivial, self-centred prediction.

If we were to leap momentarily into the future, and examine the evidence of an archaeologist or historian of, say, the twenty-second century, he or she might well assume that our entire twentieth-century culture was steered and dominated by superstition and prediction. The evidence? Popular astronomy, the Stock Exchange, horse-racing forecasts, weather forecasting, and the vast popularity of home prediction in the form of Tarot, oracles, runes, and similar prognosticating toys. Gambling in its various forms is frequently linked to predictive systems, and the entire concept of 'luck' is not merely a conditioned response, but deeply linked to our inherent belief that we can, or may, predict the fall of the dice, the turn of the card, the spin of the wheel, correctly. To say nothing, of course, of the vast strategic military computers that outguess each other towards planetary annihilation.

We may, therefore, look at specific manifestations of prophetic art and tradition through history, but these do not constitute a history of prophecy itself. The prevailing attitude of strict logic and materialist perception, in which most if not all of the arts connected to prophecy and prediction are discarded as pseudo-sciences (astrology, fortune-telling, Tarot, palmistry and so forth) has received some severe blows by advances in modern physics, biology and genetics, all of which have moved towards a holistic or interconnected universal view, supported by scientific evidence of a new order. Such holism, nodes of energy and entity within the fullness, the *pleroma*, of the universe, are the concepts at the very foundation of ancient temple arts which linger, in attenuated and often corrupt forms, into the present day as occultism or pseudo-sciences.

PROPHECY IN HISTORY

The earliest direct historical evidence for prophetic arts is probably that of Mesopotamia, between the Tigris and Euphrates rivers. The Mesopotamian cultures flourished over five thousand years ago, and Babylon in particular is famous for its development of detailed astrology. As is so often the case with a simple historical perspective, it would be misleading to suggest, as has been frequently done by single-minded writers upon many subjects, that the earliest evidence for something indicates its true origin. Although this attitude is valuable in establishing scientific disciplines, it cannot be accepted totally when we come to examine mythic, spiritual and magical traditions, as they permeate through both collective and individual consciousness in a manner which frequently defies historical perspective.

It is interesting to find that evidence from modern archaeology supports the theory of astrology, with its Assyrian origins and long history of detailed observation and annotation, as found in Cicero's classical text *De Divinatione* written during the 1st century BC. In this important text the author asserts that the Assyrians studied the patterns of the stars for over 400,000 years, and that they developed a rational science of astrology based upon the recorded effects of such observed sidereal events and patterns.

Having said that a historical perspective may be misleading, we may nevertheless assert that Babylonian astrology and related prophetic texts with an astrological basis were communicated to many centres of ancient civilisation. It seems likely that the Babylonian and Assyrian forms of astrology permeated into Egypt at an early date, and from there to Greece, Persia, India and the Far East. There is even evidence that Chinese astrology seems to owe some of its content to cuneiform texts discovered in the library of Assurbanipal, king of Nineveh.

There are, of course, alternative ways of viewing this series of connections discovered by archaeologists, linguists and researchers into ancient literature: it need not represent a dissemination from Assyria spreading ever eastwards, though this is as acceptable as any other theory based upon obscure ancient evidence – if, that is, we feel that we need a dissemination theory at all.

Esoteric tradition suggests that many of the astrological and prophetic arts actually came from even earlier civilisations, who handed their wisdom and knowledge on before their fall into oblivion: much of the 'evidence' for this lies in intuition and altered states of consciousness. There are a number of early texts and worldwide traditions that speak of the fall of great civilisations, such as Plato's *Timaeus* which describes the end of Atlantis: we shall return shortly to this text in the context of some of the more obscure but widely used theories of divination found extensively in ancient Assyrian culture.

A more direct theory is that spiritual, magical and prophetic, or the related lesser divinatory arts, retaining an enduring but variable or plastic shape and form, arise collectively within cultures whenever they reach a certain level of civilisation, of formalised perception and awareness. This mythic similarity is found worldwide, and defies a linear or disseminating perspective. (My personal opinion, for what it is worth, is that this last thesis is the only one truly viable, but that it does not preclude or deny any of the others as limited examples of cultural exchange and human historical development.)

The earliest Babylonian texts are often concerned with dream interpretation and are inextricably woven into the great poems of creation and destruction: prophecy arises in its primal state from the story of Creation: it is an aspect of Creation Myth. In the epic of Gilgamesh (c. 4000 BC) the hero dreams first of his enemy, Enkidu, then has the dream interpreted by his mother. This type of prophetic tradition, which is found worldwide, is initially of the simplest kind: a person dreams and the visions that he or she remembers relate to events that are yet to come or to events occurring at a distance. The art of divinatory or prophetic dreaming was developed to a high degree by the Greeks and Romans, and traditions involving magical sleep, special meals, visions while sleeping upon sacred sites and so forth are found throughout history and still exist today in many places.

Even the Biblical prophets gave dream interpretations, typical examples of which may be found in the Old Testament (Genesis 20: 3; 28: 12–14; 37: 4–6; 40: 12, 18; 41: 25 and many more) though astrology and similar magical arts were strictly forbidden by the developing Jewish religion, as being redolent of the civilisations of Babylon and Egypt, which were regarded as corrupt and evil. Eventually the ancient Jewish belief in the truth of dreams was confined solely to dreams connected to Yahweh, uttered or interpreted by his prophets, or by the High Priest: this comprised an important part of the development of Jewish monotheism, separating the tribes from the widespread sacrificial and divinatory arts of their neighbours and sometime conquerors. In Numbers 12: 5–6 we find:

5.   And the Lord came down in a pillar of cloud, and stood at the door of the Tent, and called both Aaron and Miriam and they both came forth.

6.   And he said, Hear now my words: if there be a prophet among you, I the Lord will make myself known unto him in a vision, I will speak with him in a dream.

PROPHECY AND KINGSHIP

Prophecy was connected in ancient Assyria (and in may other cultures) with kingship. In many early societies the king was also a priest and prophet, by nature of his kingship. The ancient Babylonians regarded a primal king, Enmeduranki, as the founder of the prophetic arts. Like many such mythic kings, he originated sets of laws, which acted as the foundations for his civilisation, and linked inseparably in many ways the prophetic arts and disciplines: he was also a powerful prophet in his own right. Divinators and interpreters of dreams and symbols were known in ancient Babylon as the Sons of Enmeduranki. Many specific sets of ancient Assyrian prophecies discovered by archaeologists bear the title of the king in whose reign they were uttered and set down in writing: thus prophecy was an instrument of statehood and kingship, forming a major part of the civic records.

This aspect of prophecy, in which it is connected to kingship and the well-being of the state, the people, and the land, is very ancient indeed, and, although it took political and often corrupt forms, it was the spiritual foundation of many great cultures. It would not be inaccurate, even from a strictly materialist historical viewpoint, to state that prophecy and its lesser variant of divination remained of major importance in the great civilisations of the world: in European history this importance persisted until at least as late as the collapse of the Roman Empire, and then in a diffuse form well into the Christian era. Many suspicious and superstitious despots well into modern times have relied upon seership, astrology and divination to bolster up their empires: we need only think of Napoleon and Hitler to find typical examples of the lust for foreknowledge being linked to the fear of losing power.

In Eastern civilisations prophecy remained at the heart of religion and of many of the rituals and structures of kingship or statecraft well into the modern era – and we should remember that the entire basis of modern Islam, the youngest of world religions, is the profound, prophetic text of the Koran.

In ancient Ireland we find a system of relationships between the king and the land, known as the divine wedding. This features in a number of Indo-European and Oriental myths and legends, and forms the deepest roots of civilisations as far apart as those of the Celts, the Chinese and the Indians. In short, the land was a sacred entity, represented usually by the image of a goddess. The king acted as husband to the land, attuned to or married to the goddess for a brief period of time: prophecy, the spiritual inspiration or uplift of a higher consciousness, was inherent in this system. Thus the king or priest-king acted as a focus or mediator for the geomantic and spiritual force: in the earliest cultures this spiritual force was usually ancestral, and we shall return to this theme wherever we trace the connections between prophecy, the Underworld, and ancestral wisdom.

While kingship was concerned with a very precise harmonising of the land and the people, focused upon the king himself but enabled through a goddess in a strongly matriarchal society, other branches of this prophetic tradition also existed. We find, for example, that poetry and prophecy were at one time inseparable: in Celtic culture this theme persists as late as the medieval *Prophecies and Life of Merlin*, to which we shall return in Chapter 8. In the following chapter we shall return to the early historical material on Assyrian prophecy and divination.

2 · ANCIENT DIVINATORY TECHNIQUES

While early Assyrian texts, intimately associated with creation myth, involved dream interpretation of the future, another style of divination was employed as major feature of state ritual. This forms a prime example of a class or type of divinatory technique found worldwide in both primitive and sophisticated cultures, though it has vanished almost entirely from modern Western forms of divination, remaining only in folkloric context in isolated regions. This method is, of course, divination by observation of bones, viscera or other bodily organs – a seemingly barbaric and totally superstitious practice.

The use of animal livers, particularly those of sheep, was widespread in Babylonian religion and state divination. This method, known as *hepatoscopy*, belongs to that class of techniques which use the interior organs of creatures to enable prophetic or divinatory insights. There are over 700 Mesopotamian examples of hepatoscopy from royal archives, and the method was well established as part of the formal religion. So fundamental was the belief in the liver as a source of divinatory enlightenment, that it remained a major organ for such arts for at least 4000 years, until the late Roman period, and probably later in isolated or secret use.

In terms of folk tradition such divination by animal organs or related means undoubtedly remained in use for many centuries into the Christian era. Folk rituals involving the use of liver or intestines, or of a boiled or scraped mutton shoulder-blade bone[7], which still persist in European and American folk custom today, are direct connections to those most ancient state rituals conducted in the civilisations of the distant past. The connection, as has been discussed above, is not a historical one of derivation or continuity, but one of protean or collective consciousness: people associated such methods with prophecy upon a very deep level, which is why they persist in rural or primal cultures but tend to vanish in modern materialist cities.

Clay models of both liver and intestines, showing presumably significant markings, have been found in ancient Babylonian and Assyrian royal library or record houses: some finds of this sort date back to very early Euphrates cultures such as that of Tel Hariri, predating that of Babylon. It seems that study of viscera and animal appearances was a highly developed art, yet with such a large number of extant records on clay tablets that deal with this subject, there is very little in the way of technical explanation or any philosophy underpinning the technique. This lack of technical explanation in surviving records has sometimes been taken to imply that the art was entirely superstitious or ignorant, but as we shall see shortly there are several possible foundations for it. It is not easy to establish whether or not hepatoscopy truly predated astrology, as both seem to have developed side by side, and both persisted for thousands of years well into the modern historical period: astrology, of course, has had an immense revival in the twentieth century, though modern astrology is different in many ways from that of the ancient world. Before moving on to more familiar ground, that of astrology, we should examine the use of body organs in prophecy and divination a little further.

Although it is a barbaric practice, and thoroughly deplorable, the widespread presence and enduring practice of using viscera for divination demands some serious attention to set it in its proper context within the arts of prophecy and divination. It is not, as has often been superficially suggested, merely an incomprehensible and whimsical art of nonsense, deceit or mystification. In spiritual terminology, it forms part of the old order of magical arts, connected to energy exchange and sacrifice, which are today replaced by the direct order of spiritual sacrifice over material: direct prophetic inspiration over projected or suppliant divination.

Even if you do not accept the existence of any higher order of natural prophecy which would render hepatoscopy or similar divinatory techniques redundant, it may be worth considering that animal sacrifice for ritual or divination was less cruel and barbaric than modern factory farming, whaling, seal hunting, or animal experimentation and abuse in the preparation of cosmetic treatments. It was also undertaken on a relatively minute scale, so it was far less destructive than modern farming and hunting methods. But whatever the argument, there seems little doubt that there are both ancient and modern practices involving animals which are unnecessary and ultimately degrading to human potential.

We may turn to Plato's *Timaeus* for a detailed and finely reasoned theory concerning the liver and viscera and modes or levels of consciousness. He states that the soul, having three parts (corresponding to the Three Worlds which we use as the basis for our general interpretation in this book: see Figure 1), had its lowest level, that of appetite, set in the belly by the gods. It was shut away from the two higher parts by the diaphragm, so that the rational soul (the highest) might work untroubled by lower appetites in its seat of existence within the head.

This theory was applied to dreams and to divination through dreams, as our quotation shows, but it also gives us insight into the philosophical, psychological and metaphysical tenets behind ancient arts such as hepatoscopy.

They knew that the lowest part would have no understanding of reason, and that it would not be in its nature to care for any rational processes of thought, should it ever get an inkling of such things; it would, they knew, be mainly led by images and phantoms, both at night and in the day-time. In consideration of this, God devised for it a thing so constituted as the liver, and placed this in the region tenanted by the lowest part of the Soul, a thing, by God's contrivance, compact, smooth, shining, with both a sweet and a bitter quality, in order that it might be like a mirror which receives the shapes of things and offers images to the view, and that thereby the thoughts coming down from the Mind, reflected in it, might have power to daunt it, whenever they made use of any part of its native bitterness and bore upon it in a stern and threatening way, subtly curdling, as it were, the liver throughout, so that it might present bilious colours, drawing it all together and making it wrinkled and rough. In regard to the lobe, the biliary ducts and the orifices, here they would bend something out of the straight and contract, there they would bring about obstruction and congestion, and so cause pains and feelings of malaise. At another time a gentle wafture from the Mind would produce pictures of the opposite sort; unwilling to agitate or to make connexion with what is of contrary nature to itself, it would afford a respite from bitterness and would use for this purpose the sweetness which is native to the liver and adjust everything, make everything smooth and free, and so cause the portion of the Soul lodged round about the liver to be at peace with itself and happy. Thus at night this part of the Soul passes the time temperately, engaging in divination during sleep, incapable as it is of participating in reason and thought. For the gods who constructed us, mindful of their Father's charge, when He bade them fashion the mortal kind as good as its nature allowed, made a success even of our worser part, and, in order that it might in some way get an apprehension of truth, established therein the seat of divination. It is a sufficient proof that God coupled divination with human witlessness, that no one in his sober senses sets about divination of the really inspired sort, but either in sleep, when the intellectual faculties are tied up, or in an abnormal state through disease or some kind of 'enthusiasm.' On the other hand, it belongs to the sane intelligence to construe the words heard, in dream or in a waking state, by the person of divining enthusiastic temperament, and discriminate by rational calculation the phantoms such a person has seen, to determine what they mean, and to whom good or evil is signified as coming, or as having come in the past, or as attaching in the present. Whilst the person remains in the state of madness, it is not his business to interpret the apparition he sees or the cries he himself makes, but the old saying is true, that it belongs to the sane man alone to do and know his own business and himself. Hence the custom has come about of setting the kind of people called *prophetai*, as interpreters, over the utterances of inspired madness. Sometimes one hears the name of 'diviners (*manteis*)' extended to such interpreters also, but that is to show ignorance of the whole matter; the people described are like actors, who render to the public the things which, as uttered and seen, are riddling symbols; they are not themselves diviners but are most properly described as the 'prophets' of the diviners. This then is the reason why the liver has the nature which it has, and why it was put to grow in the place we have stated, for the sake of divination. So long as the individual is alive the indications given by the liver are clearer; but when life has departed the liver becomes blind, and the signs it gives are too indistinct to yield any plain direction.

(Plato, *Timaeus*, 71a–72b)

There is no way of establishing, today, if this complex theory was generated by Plato to explain existing beliefs and practices concerning the relationship between certain organs and consciousness, handed down from ancient times, or if it was a detailed exposition of an enduring tradition. If the second is the case, then it gives us a number of grounds for animal sacrifice and the study of viscera: the simple minds of the lower creatures, having no higher reason, were open, in a dreamlike, non-rational manner to the subtle forces of the cosmos, normally perceived by humans only in occasional dreams and requiring interpretation. Thus the patterns of future events might be found imprinted upon animal livers, just as the human liver was the organ of such consciousness in humanity. Only in much later centuries did medicine abandon similar theories, and finally stand them upon their head, concluding that imbalance of the stomach or liver or other organs could cause strange dreams!

There is, however, another enduring theory concerning the relationship between natural patterns and divination, and this is perhaps the true foundation of all of the foregoing and of all divinatory and prophetic techniques. Ancient augurers not only used to cut open animals, but simply observed selected creatures, their shape, their movements, and the times at which they did certain things. Flights of birds, patterns of smoke, swirling waters, the movement of trees in the wind or of ants upon a twig, all were regarded as potentially prophetic. Why might this be so?

We can take two basic viewpoints, the first being that it was simple superstition. This view is supported by certain schools of modern materialist studies of the psyche, in which imbalance causes individuals to ascribe meaning to events where no inherent meaning is truly present. This can range from simple but illogical ascription of significance, something with which we are all familiar, to highly imbalanced and potentially dangerous delusions based upon surrounding events, patterns, people, and what are in truth perfectly innocent occurrences. The first category, that of ascribing meaning to trivia, is found within all of us to a greater or lesser extent: it is formalised in popular superstition – the lucky black cat, blessings when you sneeze, and the wide range of differing personal good- or bad-luck attributes that individuals (often secretly) believe in. This harmless level may indeed be connected to the ancient art of augury, as we shall see shortly.

When the mildly irrational use of connective events becomes obsessive or demanding or a major feature of life, it has spilled over into dangerous imbalance, and this potential imbalance was clearly recognised in the ancient world just as it is today. There is a quite false tendency, reinforced by poorly written history books, that the ancients were imbued with utterly spurious, frivolous and time-wasting divinatory obsessions: in fact the rational argument for and against such arts was a constant debate from the earliest times, and persisted actively through every era, just as it does today. In an ancient Assyrian text concerning the good or ill of a typical city, we find that a city will perish if it has too many divinators and interpreters, but is likely to prosper if it has many doves and fools. This is one of the earliest contradistinctions between divination by art and divination by nature, as described and discussed in depth by Cicero in the first century BC in his *De Divinatione*. Many modern books are published yearly which deal exactly with this same topic, as if it were something startlingly new and original to compare intuition, divination arts, and the rational disciplines of science. No doubt it formed street conversation in ancient Babylon.

Setting aside gradations of mental imbalance connected to significant events, we find the ancient theory of holism restated in modern psychology by C. G. Jung as synchronicity, to contain many implications for the methods of divination or prophecy employed in early cultures. Furthermore we have the surprising support of modern mathematics, biology, and physics, where it is becoming increasingly clear that the vibration of a butterfly wing or the falling of a leaf may be inextricably linked, for example, with changes in the entire weather pattern for the planet. In other words, all energies and entities, all beings, are interwoven. The universe is a fullness, a *pleroma* in which nodes or power patterns arise, interact, and transform.

Thus a seer, possessed of a natural (but often highly trained) ability to judge such interactions, might observe a simple natural event, such as the flow of smoke in the wind, or the flight of birds, and draw conclusions regarding apparently unrelated future or distant events. This concept of holism and interconnection immediately shifts the practices of the ancient world into a new perspective.

The relationship between divination by art and divination by nature is important in this context, for the true or natural prophet or seer does not rationalise what he or she concludes from observing the holism of the surrounding environment or certain highlighted events within it. There is no concept of a systematised observation, but of an intuitive higher mode of consciousness, in which the 'answer' simply arises as a result of observing the chosen means of augury, or, more interestingly in our present context, as a spontaneous and unexpected event triggered by a certain pattern, shape, being, or movement in the natural surroundings. If we referred this entirely to divination by art, the individual would have to rely on long sets of symbolic attributes for every potential event: this technique also played its part in the ancient world, and is, of course, found in many forms even today. Most techniques of divination usually combine both art and nature, sets of symbols and the intuition.

My personal viewpoint on this subject is as follows: every individual has the natural prophetic ability; we usually call it intuition. I am emphatically not referring here to clairvoyance, psychism, or telepathy – these are all explanatory or reductionist terms used to offer us a secondary and often spurious level of seeming understanding. In the holism of the environment – the planet, of which we are an inseparable part – certain patterns speak to or resonate within our intuitive or non-linear (that is, illogical) consciousness.

Very often this interconnective situation enables us simply to know what has or will come to pass. For most of us this either does not manifest at all, or is filtered through our general modes of conditioned thought and emotion. In some cases it breaks through very strongly, whether we like it or not.

The intuition may be heightened to detect the levels of consciousness or any insight or revelation. St Augustine, who wrote so much that bridged the pagan and early Christian spiritual disciplines, described how his mother said 'she could, through a certain feeling, which in words she could not express, discern between Divine revelations, and the dreams of her own soul' (Confessions, vi: 13). While the seer or seeress may develop this unerring intuition concerning divine revelation, it is judged by its fruits within the community, or more confusedly by the hindsight of later generations.

Primitive examples of techniques to utilise this perception of holism may help us to grasp the subject, for they do not have massive lists of intellectual attributes typical to city-based civilisations. For example, certain sacred patterns, such as those of the American Indian or the Australian aborigine, enable people to travel vast distances over unmapped territories (a wonder to the technological European mind) or to establish knowledge at a distance simply by studying a few seemingly random swirls in sand or on stone. It seems likely that the sacred cup and ring marks and spirals of the megalithic culture, incised upon standing stones and burial chambers, were used in a similar way.

ASTROLOGY AND PROPHECY

We may now return briefly to the much discussed art of astrology – but we are not going to embark upon a general discussion or yet another tedious 'proof' or 'refutation' of astrology. All of that category of writing and thought is irrelevant: if you accept that astrology has something to tell us, as did, for example, C. G. Jung, one of the founding fathers of the materialist technique of psychotherapy, then it must be upon a level beyond the trivial, popularised nonsense of the tabloid newspapers. The concept of a pleroma or holism, a fullness in which nodes of energy interact with one another, in which creation and de-creation are simultaneous events, tends to obviate both intellectual nitpicking and idle superstition.

What is important is that any well-balanced pattern, be it simple or complex, will be sufficient to trigger our deeper levels of perception. Any pattern will suffice, providing we work in an as honest and disciplined manner as possible. The other very important proviso, central to both materialist sciences and mystical disciplines, is that we should not flit from art to art, science to science, art to science, in a trivial or dilettante manner: any set of patterns must be followed through to its ultimate conclusion, which is, paradoxically, liberation from the patterns themselves.

This is no mystical or obscure statement, for each age, each civilisation, has been based upon 'truths' or 'systems' which have been superseded: the validity is not in any system itself, but in working with it to find a way towards truth.

EARLY ASTROLOGY

A definition of astrology, and its origins, as practised in the classical period and influencing Roman religion is found in Franz Cumont's important study *Oriental Religions in Roman Paganism* (1911).

The fundamental dogma of astrology, as conceived by the Greeks, was that of universal solidarity. The world is a vast organism, all the parts of which are connected through an unceasing exchange of molecules of effluvia. The stars, inexhaustible generators of energy, constantly act upon the earth and man – upon man, the epitome of all nature, a 'microcosm' whose every element corresponds to some part of the starry sky. This was, in a few words, the theory formulated by the Stoic disciples of the Chaldeans; but if we divest it of all the philosophic garments

38

with which it has been adorned, what do we find? The idea of sympathy, a belief as old as human society! The savage peoples also established mysterious relations between all bodies and all the beings that inhabit the earth and the heavens, and which to them were animated with a life of their own endowed with latent power, but we shall speak of this later on, when taking up the subject of magic. Even before the propagation of the Oriental religions, popular superstition in Italy and Greece attributed a number of odd actions to the sun, the moon, and the constellations as well.

The Chaldaei, however, claimed a predominant power for the stars. In fact, they were regarded as gods *par excellence* by the religion of the ancient Chaldeans in its beginnings. The sidereal religion of Babylon concentrated deity, one might say, in the luminous moving bodies at the expense of other natural objects, such as stones, plants, animals, which the primitive Semitic faith considered equally divine. The stars always retained this character, even at Rome. They were not, as to us, infinitely distant bodies moving in space according to the inflexible laws of mechanics, and whose chemical composition may be determined. To the Latins as to the Orientals, they were propitious or baleful deities, whose ever-changing relations determined the events of this world.

The sky, whose unfathomable depth had not yet been perceived, was peopled with heroes and monsters of contrary passions, and the struggle above had an immediate echo upon earth. By what principle have such a quality and so great an influence been attributed to the stars? Is it for reasons derived from their apparent motion and known through observation or experience? Sometimes. Saturn made people apathetic and irresolute, because it moved most slowly of all the planets. But in most instances purely mythological reasons inspired the precepts of astrology. The seven planets were associated with certain deities, Mars, Venus, or Mercury, whose character and history are known to all. It is sufficient simply to pronounce their names to call to mind certain personalities that may be expected to act according to their natures, in every instance. It was natural for Venus to favor lovers, and for Mercury to assure the success of business transactions and dishonest deals. The same applies to the constellations, with which a number of legends are connected: 'catasterism' or translation into the stars, became the natural conclusion of a great many tales. The heroes of mythology, or even those of human society, continued to live in the sky in the form of brilliant stars. There Perseus again met Andromeda, and the Centaur Chiron, who is none other than Sagittarius, was on terms of good fellowship with the Dioscuri.

These constellations, then, assumed to a certain extent the good and the bad qualities of the mythical or historical beings that had been transferred upon them. For instance, the serpent, which shines near the northern pole, was the author of medical cures, because it was the animal sacred to Æsculapius.

The religious foundation of the rules of astrology, however, can not always be recognized. Sometimes it is entirely forgotten, and in such cases the rules assume the appearance of axioms, or of laws based upon long observation of celestial phenomena. Here we have a simple aspect of science. The process of assimilation with the gods and catasterism were known in the Orient long before they were practiced in Greece.

The traditional outlines that we reproduce on our celestial maps are the fossil remains of a luxuriant mythological vegetation, and besides our classic sphere the ancients knew another, the 'barbarian' sphere, peopled with a world of fantastic persons and animals. These sidereal monsters, to whom powerful qualities were ascribed, were likewise the remnants of a multitude of forgotten beliefs. Zoolatry was abandoned in the temples, but people continued to regard as divine the lion, the bull, the bear, and the fishes, which the Oriental imagination had seen in the starry vault. Old totems of the Semitic tribes or the Egyptian divisions lived again, transformed into constellations. Heterogeneous elements, taken from all the religions of the Orient, were combined in the uranography of the ancients, and in the power ascribed to the phantoms that it evoked, vibrates in the indistinct echo of ancient devotions that are often completely unknown to us.

Astrology, then, was religious in its origin and in its principles. It was religious also in its close relation to the Oriental religions, especially those of the Syrian Baals and of Mithra; finally, it was religious in the effects that it produced. I do not mean the effects expected from a constellation in any particular instance: as for example the power to evoke the gods that were subject to their domination. But I have in mind the general influence those doctrines exercised upon Roman paganism.

When the Olympian gods were incorporated among the stars, when Saturn and Jupiter became planets and the celestial virgin a sign of the zodiac, they assumed a character very different from the one they had originally possessed. It has been shown how, in Syria, the idea of an infinite repetition of cycles of years according to which the celestial revolutions took place, led to the conception of divine eternity, how the theory of a fatal domination of the stars over the earth brought about that of the omnipotence of the 'lord of the heavens,' and how the introduction of a universal religion was the necessary result of the belief that the stars exerted an influence upon the peoples of every climate. The logic of all these consequences of the principles of astrology was plain to the Latin as well as to the Semitic races, and caused a rapid transformation of the ancient idolatry. As in Syria, the sun, which the astrologers called the leader of the planetary choir, 'who is established as king and leader of the whole world,' necessarily became the highest power of the Roman pantheon.

> (Franz Cumont, *Oriental Religions in Roman Paganism* (1911), pp. 171–5)

Early Babylonian astrology was concerned with weather – and though this might seem to be an obvious requirement in early cultures where rain or drought meant the difference between life or death, we find the connection between astrology and weather perpetuated right through into the Middle Ages, when the *Prophecies and Life of Merlin* (to which we shall return on page 93) linked weather with originative and divine powers, as harmonics of the holistic universe. One category of Babylonian astrology, *adad*, was named after the weather deity who ruled storms, lightning, and rainfall. We find this link between divinities of natural energy, such as lightning and wind, and prophecy, perpetuated in later figures such as Zeus, Odin, Yahweh, and many more.

Babylonian religion placed great emphasis upon the Moon as a major divinity, and, like many early cultures, the calendar was primarily lunar. But the famous ziggurats, which stood by the Babylonian temples, were used to study the Moon, Sun and planets, by direct observation. The sophisticated Zodiac, as used in modern astrology, was not fully present in early Babylonian astrology, but an observational framework, based upon the concept of the sphere of the Six Directions (Above, Below, East, South, West, North). The active, rapidly moving planets were known as *bibbu*, or wild goats, while the slower moving 'fixed' stars were referred to as *tame*. In this simple framework, the appearance or non-appearance of certain planets in zones of the sky or over horizon points were said to cause good or ill fortune due to their direct influence upon human endeavour.

This is an extension of the holism of weather prediction: the patterns or interactions of the planets or planetary gods and goddesses resonate right through to the human world and have certain effects. Whether it is true or not, we find in Roman literature a classical tradition that the Assyrians accumulated observations and details of synchronous events over many thousands of years, establishing a detailed art of astrological correlation and therefore of potentially accurate prediction.

CHINESE ASTROLOGY

Primal astrology is also found in China, at least as early as 3000 BC. Confucius, writing around 500 BC said, 'Heaven sends down its good or evil symbols, and wise men act accordingly.' As in ancient Babylon, astrology formed part of the complex structure of government, with many stellar attributes connected directly to court offices and functions. Court astrologers who failed to predict solar eclipses, for example, were likely to be executed, and one emperor blamed his own maladministration for an unpredicted eclipse. This implies, interestingly, a belief in a two-way interaction between human activities and stellar or planetary events.

The concept of harmonic attributes, sequences of interrelated arts and sciences, was highly developed in Chinese astrology: this celestial and terrestrial harmony resonated through orders or sequences of sacred music, totem or sacred animals, divinities, and stellar and planetary bodies. In the thirteenth century Marco Polo gave a famous description of the use of the Lo King, a disc of concentric circles of harmonic correlations, used for predictions and determination of fortunate dates for civic and private acts. According to Marco Polo the burial or cremation of high officials was decided astrologically, and corpses were left until appropriate planetary patterns were in the ascendant.

All of this ceremonial astrology is of the category of divination by art, in which increasing attention to details and formalism, often linked to political function, replaces the random and inspirational prophetic event. But the use of the astrological chart, the master glyph such as the Lo King, and other systems, still includes that random potential of intuition or higher realisation, through its deeper use in meditative and visualising disciplines.

CLASSICAL DEFINITIONS OF PROPHECY

An important classical text on the prophetic and divinatory experience of the ancient world is Cicero's *De Divinatione*, in two books, written during the first century BC. Much of the defence of divination in Cicero is based upon the Platonic/Stoic writings of Posidonius of Apamea in Syria (c 135–150 BC.) who may have been an actual teacher of Cicero, and whose writings had a powerful influence upon the development of Roman theology. We find that the distinction between divination by art and divination by nature, which is discussed throughout this book, was well established among the classical philosophers.

According to Cicero/Posidonius, divination by art included reading of portents and signs, astrology, and other types of divination with a technical apparatus or vocabulary that required intellectual interpretation or systematic study and training. Divination by nature, however, was an inherent faculty of human consciousness, an enlightenment or enhancement perception that occurred of its own will.

Astrology is given a clear historical perspective in this text, as being based upon the observations of the Babylonians or Assyrians over a period of almost 500,000 years. This was a scientific art, not involved with transpersonal awareness or illumination. Certain signs and patterns were known, through the long observations of the Assyrians, to lead to certain types of event or situation.

Ancient philosophers, particularly those of the Peripatetic school, frequently rejected art divination as being unproven, a mere fabrication not supported by logic. But they accepted natural divination, dream consciousness, prophetic utterances, even though it was customary for state oracle in Greece to have expert interpreters, the *exegetai*. The Sceptics, however, tended to be in favour of rejecting both art and natural divination, as the argument against the falsities of art divination tended to collapse when it was still customary to apply mental systems (art divination) to interpret the mysterious utterance of the Sybil or the images of dreams.

IAMBLICHUS

The pure utterance of prophecy is a rare event, and inevitably bound up within the cultural medium of the land of the prophet or sybil. There are a number of distinct streams of belief, practice, and practical instruction connected to prophecy and the lesser divinatory arts: some of these remain active today, particularly astrology. In some religious movements or cults, such as those that fuse old chthonic magic with a formal religion (Tibetan Buddhism being a major example, or inspirational Christian sects that utter in tongues being minor examples), the entire population of the universe is defined and certain entities may be summoned, or alternatively appear of their own volition, in the context of divination or prophecy.

In *De Mysteriis Egyptorum*, the work of Iamblichus written in the fourth century AD, we find a very precise description of the orders of supernatural beings. This text, incidentally, seems to have influenced the prophetic development of Nostradamus, as his own techniques of attaining vision (see page 84) are drawn, in part, from Iamblichus.

In modern magical or esoteric arts the orders or hierarchies of supernatural beings are frequently called inner world beings, though this tends to imply, quite falsely, that they are merely constructions of the imagination. In most ancient cultures – and indeed in many ethnic magical and religious practices today – many of the levels or types of entity described in this passage appear, though the names, of course, vary from culture to culture, and the definition must always be by function. Functional definition is very important in magical divinatory and prophetic events or arts, and one of the great deluding aspects of such arts is the tendency for students to become entirely enmeshed in names and categories, without ever finding the true functions of the beings that they seek to contact. In *De Mysteriis* (ii: 4) we find this comprehensive description of the otherworldly beings, which fits well with divinatory and invocatory practices from the most ancient times to the present day. The author is discussing *epiphanies*, the appearance of supernatural beings:

in the case of *gods* and *goddesses* they sometimes cover the whole sky and the sun and the moon, while the earth can no longer remain steady when they descend. When *archangels* appear, certain portions of the world are agitated, and their arrival is heralded by a divided light. The archangels differ in magnitude according to the size of the provinces over which they rule. *Angels* are distinguished by smaller size, and by their being divided numerically. In the case of *daemones* the division goes further, and their magnitudes visibly fluctuate. *Heroes* are of a smaller appearance, but of a greater majesty of bearing. Of the *archons* the most powerful belonging to the outer region of the cosmos are large and massive in appearance. Those, on the other hand, who undergo division in the region of matter are apt to be boastful and generate illusions. *Souls* are not equal in size, but are generally smaller in appearance than heroes.

Next let us define the distinctions between the appearances of those beings who make themselves manifest. In the case of gods, what is seen is clearer than truth itself; every detail shines out exactly and its articulations are shown in brilliant light. The appearances of archangels are still true and full. Those of angels maintain the same character, but their being is not expressed in the image seen with the same fullness (as that of archangels). Those of daemones are blurred, and even more blurred are those of heroes. In the case of archons those who are cosmic powers are clearly perceived, but those who are involved in matter are blurred. Yet both give an impression of power, whereas the appearance of souls is merely shadowy.

And here is Iamblichos on Divine Possession:

People in this state [he says] have either submitted their whole physical life, as a vehicle or an instrument, to the gods who inspire them, or they substitute a Divine life for their human life, or they act in virtue of their own proper life, but addressed to the god. They do not act 'consciously,' nor are they 'awake,' nor do they themselves 'get a hold upon the future,' nor are they moved like those whose activities follow volitions, nor have they consciousness of what they themselves are doing – not only not their 'ordinary consciousness' but no consciousness at all, nor do they direct their own understanding to themselves, nor is any of the knowledge they put forth their own. . . . It is wrong to conceive of enthusiasm as an operation of the soul, or of any faculty in the soul, mind or energies. Divine possession is not a human work at all, nor does it depend upon the parts and energies of man. Those parts and energies are there indeed as a substratum, and the god uses them as instruments, but the whole work of divination he accomplishes through his own agency; acting freely in separation from everything else, without any movement of the human soul or human body, he is active by himself. Where the soothsaying is directed in the way I describe, it is infallible. But when the soul is in a state of unrest beforehand, or begins to move during the process, or becomes involved in the movements of the body, and so disturbs the divine harmony, the deliverances become turbid and false, and the 'enthusiasm' is no longer of the true kind, not genuinely divine.

De Mysteriis, iii: 4ff

HAS PROPHECY DEVELOPED OR CHANGED?

The short answer to this is probably no: the complex foundations definable from ancient cultures are exactly those employed in prophecy and prediction from the medieval period to the present day. The sole important difference, which has been discussed in the Introduction, is the appearance of electronic-calculation devices, which serve to make forecasts within the limits of their data, and so replace certain aspects of forecasting and prediction that were originally a property of consciousness. When we come to a discussion of techniques (Chapter 3) we find that certain of the ancient methods, such as animal sacrifice and divine possession, are no longer valid or desirable. Such atavistic prophetic techniques serve only to devolve us, so we might suggest that in this sense there has been a certain degree of evolution of human awareness in the divinatory, predictive and prophetic arts.

3 · A SHORT
DEFINITION
OF PROPHECY

Although we have a complex of interlinked definitions and connections throughout this book, ranging through prediction, divination, farsight, insight, and prophecy itself, it is worth isolating a short and precise definition of prophecy in its purest form. To reach this definition we may draw upon the entire range of historical examples and concepts related to prophecy. First we should remove the lower harmonics of divination and related arts or abilities, for these are not truly prophetic: they deal mainly with transitory or even trivial matters. Astrology in its modern form does not constitute a prophetic art, but ancient astrology which was linked to direct observation and intuitions or meditation upon the visible stars and planets forms a middle ground between divinatory arts and pure prophecy.

The term pure prophecy is not used here in a formal dogmatic religious sense, favouring one set of beliefs over another, but in a strict sense of something unmixed with other arts, details, supportive tools and so forth. Pure prophecy is a property of, or event arising within, spiritual consciousness, an inspiration that flows directly into the human vehicle and causes utterance of truth. What form such utterances take is generally moulded by tradition, for prophets work within specific spiritual or cultural traditions. These traditions give a symbolic language and content that may, in some cases, connect to astrology (of the ancient type) or to orthodox religious beliefs, texts, and customs such as those of the Biblical prophets. It is also worth remembering that in certain early civilizations, such as those of Assyria, astrology was in itself an important feature of the orthodox state religion, linked to the formal worship of the planetary and stellar deities.

We may build our definition a little further by considering historical examples of prophecy: the first feature that appears is that prophecy is always, without exception, connected to a mythic tradition, and to a specific land. The application of prophetic texts to general world events is a very recent phase or craze; any unbiased strict analysis of prophetic texts through history and worldwide soon shows that they are first and foremost concerned with the land and people in which the prophecies originated. Wider historical events are only touched upon when they impinge directly upon the native land and its people: this environmental quality is typical to, for example, Greek, Hebrew, Celtic, and American Indian prophecies, most of which have been published in various forms. Some typical examples of prophecies are found in our later chapters.

The second feature of true prophecy is that it leaps directly from the land and people, through a mythic or religious symbolic language, to the stars, or in the case of a monotheistic cult, to godhead. The highest divinity, the universal Being (be it God or Goddess or Living Spirit) manifests through prophetic inspiration, and pours truth through the mouth of the prophet. He or she utters unconsciously, for the higher awareness has suspended the individual ego, but the prophetic impulse nevertheless uses the mythic or religious language of the prophet's land and people. Furthermore the events, warnings, blessings, imprecations and implications are all couched in terms of the native land and its people, and talk not of individual short-term matters, but of deeply transformative and important major events. The imagery may then take an octave leap into the stars, or form a declaration of divine vision.

This brings us to the third feature of true prophecy which is utterance of cosmic vision, of mystical cosmology. Such utterances, often but not always connected to primal astrology, act as sacred texts. They are the guiding sources for those who seek to tread the hard road of inner transformation through mystical religious meditative or magical techniques. They may eventually become part of dogmatic political manipulations, as has happened to the profound prophecies of the Islamic, Hebraic or Christian religions, or they may pass underground to become the hidden remnant of ancient world-views and shamanistic or magical arts, preserved in song, verse, or oral tuition.

Intellectual, creative, or fashionable revivals such as those of the Renaissance or the Victorian and Edwardian period, or indeed, that of the present-day New Age enthusiasm, perpetuate interest in old prophetic texts, which were originally written out from purely oral utterances.

Prophecy is, of course, always oral. The written text comes later, usually set out from verses learned by heart, and perhaps at many removes from the original prophetic experience, for by this time they are already part of mystical or religious tradition that has diffused itself through the land of origin. The exception to this oral diffusion is found when, as in Assyrian, Babylonian or Greek state prophecies, scribes wrote out the utterance of the seer or sybil immediately, according to a well-established management system.

The reasons for prophecy being essentially oral are important to our definition; historically we might assume that prophecy was oral because it arose in early cultures with little or no literacy. This is disproven by the examples mentioned above from civilisations in which prophecy played a major role, and to this of course we can add other examples such as ancient Egypt, India, Tibet, or China. These all had profound and enduring prophetic traditions connected directly to the state and its religion in various ways: prophecies were frequently noted and preserved in sacred books. The Holy Quran is another significant example of an originally oral prophetic set of verse being set into a literary form as part of an orthodox religion. So the oral nature of prophecy is not a matter of lack of available reduction or general literacy.

Prophecy is oral because it suspends many of the regular functions of ego-consciousness: more simply, a prophet cannot prophesy and write at the same time. Hence the well-known practice of having scribes attend ancient oracles: we might cynically add that the scribes were well able to modify what they were hearing and interpret it according to a current political climate, and that there is evidence of this type of modification in many examples, such as from the oracle of Delphi and from those of Babylon. But as we are concerned with pure prophecy, we will consider only a situation where the scribe accurately writes whatever the prophet or sybil utters.

Anyone who has experience in meditation will agree that even the earlier stages of altered consciousness tend to suspend the ability to write. Poets have described this situation, where the inspiration flies far ahead of the physical pen, and many hours of skill and retrospective labour are need to create a final vehicle for the poetic reality that originally occurred. Poetry is closely linked to prophecy, though we might exclude some modern self-styled poets, who are really only good entertainers or comedians.

In certain cultures, however, the art of memory was considered to be an essential requirement of the prophet or poet. The Celts are perhaps the most famous example of this, for in druidic lore the written word hardly existed until relatively late into the Roman period of conquest in Gaul and Britain. In Celtic countries, truly immense sets of verses, lore knowledge, genealogies, epic and prophetic or mythic tales, were all preserved by memory alone. So conservative (in the true sense of the word) was this oral tradition, that when early Christian monastics wrote out Irish epic oral poetry, the culture described was that of the Bronze Age.[7]

By the medieval period we have a number of interesting Celtic prophetic texts, ascribed to Merlin. In the twelfth-century *Vita Merlini* we find Merlin watching the stars in a specially constructed building, with a large number of attendant scribes who write down his utterances. This, of course, harks back to a classical tradition, but may also be connected to the use of megalithic sites, and Merlin's traditional link to Stonehenge which legend asserts he caused to be brought from Ireland by magical means.

MERLIN'S OBSERVATORY

(His Sister Ganieda seeks to restrain Merlin from returning to the woods, and he agrees that his mode of life should change. He requests her to build an Observatory, with a house for winter shelter, where he can watch the stars and have detailed notes taken by scribes. He spends the Summer close to nature, but the Winter in the Observatory.)

After these things had happened the prophet was making haste to go to the woods he was accustomed to, hating the people in the city. The queen advised him to stay with her and to put off his desired trip to the woods until the cold of white winter, which was then at hand, should be over, and summer should return again with its tender fruits on which he could live while the weather grew warm from the sun. He refused, and desirous of departing and scorning the winter he said to her,

'O dear sister, why do you labor to hold me back? Winter with his tempests cannot frighten me, nor icy Boreas when he rages with his cruel blasts and suddenly injures the flocks of sheep with hail; neither does Auster disturb me when its rain clouds shed their waters. Why should I not seek the deserted groves and the green woodlands? Content with a little I can endure the frost. There under the leaves of the trees among the odorous blossoms I shall take pleasure in lying through the summer; but lest I lack food in winter you might build me a house in the woods and have servants in it to wait on me and prepare me food when the ground refuses to produce grain or the trees fruit. Before the other buildings build me a remote one with seventy doors and as many windows through which I may watch fire-breathing Phoebus and Venus and the stars gliding from the heavens by night, all of whom shall show me what is going to happen to the people of the kingdom. And let the same number of scribes be at hand, trained to take my dictation, and let them be attentive to record my prophecy on their tablets. You too are to come often, dear sister, and then you can relieve my hunger with food and drink.' After he had finished speaking he departed hastily for the woods.

His sister obeyed him and built the place he had asked for, and the other houses and whatever else he had bid her. But he, while the apples remained and Phoebus was ascending higher through the stars, rejoiced to remain beneath the leaves and to wander through the groves with their soothing breezes. Then winter came, harsh with icy winds, and despoiled the ground and the trees of all their fruit, and Merlin lacked food because the rains were at hand, and he came, sad and hungry, to the aforesaid place. Thither the queen often came and rejoiced to bring her brother both food and drink. He, after he had refreshed himself with various kinds of edibles, would arise and express his approval of his sister. Then wandering about the house he would look at the stars while he prophesied things like these which he knew were going to come to pass.

(Quoted in R. J. Stewart, *The Mystic Life of Merlin* (1989), pp. 97–8).

A fourth feature of prophecy is that it is generally concerned with spiritual or ethical instruction: much of the true prophetic utterance concerns right living. This is not simply a matter of strict spiritual elders castigating their wanton flock of souls, as we are often led to believe in orthodox religions, but has a very profound origin indeed.

Prophetic consciousness or vision and its utterance seeks to affirm and declare the presence of universal Being, of divinity in the world of humanity. The divinity may take the form of the Great Goddess, as in the oracles of Isis, or of Apollo, as in the oracle at Delphi, or it may take the form of the single ultimate Divinity that transcends and subsumes all others, as in the Holy Quran.

Whatever the tradition or form, prophecy seek to state rightness, balance, harmony, and a union or proper relationship between the human soul, the land, the planet, and ultimately the universe. Little wonder, therefore, that prophets spent much of their energy in uttering prescriptions for spiritual health, warnings of potential disasters, divine demands for proper living, sanctity of life, preservation and empowering of the environment, loving one's neighbour, and so forth.

In this fourth category we may also add an important subset, which is that of revolution. Prophecy is frequently revolutionary: it seeks to demolish the old corrupt order and replace it with a new vision, a new spiritual rule in the material world. This urge can, and often does, become corrupted in turn into religious or millennial politics; its origin however, is in that radical revivifying power, the ever vivid and new awareness of spiritual life, of divinity, of truth, that cuts across all coagulated stagnant conditions and destroys them, only in order to renew.

A fifth feature of true or pure prophecy is that much of the prophetic lore handed down to us by religious or esoteric traditions is about destruction, apocalyptic vision, new orders of universal creation. Here we leap once again into the cosmic octave, for the revolution becomes not a matter of regional or world politics, but of stellar reality. The revolution is universal, and the worldly events are tiny reflections of stellar potencies. Here we may return again to the intimate connection between prophecy and creation myth, for the apocalyptic vision is the end of the Great Story, the final turning of the Wheel of Creation.

The harmonic nature of this revelation is very well represented in Tarot, where we find the trumps of Fortune, Justice, and Judgement declaring three levels or harmonics of fate.[8] The Wheel of Fortune reveals the outer conditions of ceaseless change in life: the Wheel of Justice reveals a higher octave of these forces, in terms of anabolic and catabolic energies, usually concerned with the inner condition or soul. The Wheel of Judgement, also known variously as the Last Trump, the Last Judgement, the Apocalypse, reveals the universal judgement, the ultimate polarity of creation and destruction.

This triple pattern is traditionally represented by three female figures, known in the classical and pagan world as the goddesses Fortune, Justice, and Wisdom (Judgement). They manifest as Fortuna, Minerva or Athena, and the Great Goddess, plus of course many other forms in various cultures. These feminine archetypes are, traditionally, the patronesses or inspirers of prophecy. Even in monotheistic religions the traces of feminine divine power are present in various hidden but definable forms.

PROPHETIC TECHNIQUES

We have discussed the historic spectrum of prophetic techniques and traditions throughout this book, but certain basic aspects may be singled out, either in the context of methods to be avoided, or in the context of methods that might be suitable for the psyche of the twenty-first century.

Firstly it must be strongly argued that ancient techniques of divine possession, such as those connected to the oracle of the Sybil, in which a potent god and goddess form supplants the psyche of the seer are not suitable for contemporary humanity. We may set aside, for the present, the major discussion of the reality of such psychic displacement, and whether or not it is a true prophetic experience or merely a type of mental imbalance. Even if such techniques are true communications from god-forms, and certainly the ancients believed that they were so, and made clear distinctions between insanity and divine possession and inspiration, they have no place in the present day.

The key note of spiritual techniques is not reversion to outmoded temple techniques in which the individual soul is subservient or even agonised by the god or goddess form. The individual, or indeed the meditative or visualising group, today works upon a higher spiral of consciousness, yet often with the same images and energies as might have been found in an ancient Mystery or temple or religion. In other words the individual soul should not be enslaved or displaced, but rather act in harmony with the archetypes, divinities, and higher octaves of consciousness that form part of a transpersonal or spiritual tradition.

It is perhaps significant that spiritualist mediumship, which superficially seems to use similar techniques to those of the ancient sybilline oracles, can only provide trivia and gossip. Perhaps the use of mediumistic displacement of the ego or of the individual soul no longer attunes to the more potent levels of consciousness; we discussed elsewhere the differences between ancient temple techniques of divine possession, and the modern role of mediumship. In all such comparisons we may set aside, albeit temporarily, any judgement as to fraud, delusion, alternative reality, or true spiritual insight. In spiritualist mediumship we often find that all four are mingled together so closely that they are hard to separate.

Yet anyone seeking the clarity of higher octaves of consciousness, at the states or levels where prophetic inspiration has always been said to abide, and to resonate this expanded consciousness through into more habitual levels of awareness, must always aim for true insight and heightened reality, and ruthlessly strip away all tendencies to fraud, acting, delusion, and self-deceit.

FACTORS AND METHODS OF PROPHETIC INSPIRATION

Rather than expand upon any specific system, it might be valuable to provide here some general hints and a few specific guidelines and aids towards inspirational or prophetic consciousness. The first and last and perennial key to such consciousness is that it is founded upon strict self-discipline, and framed within a clearly defined spiritual tradition. Anything wilful, fantastical, or vague, cannot, by its very nature, lead to prophetic consciousness. There is, however, a hallowed tradition of the mad prophet living precariously in the wildwood or desert: we find this in Old Testament texts and other Semitic traditions, and it is strongly emphasised in the Merlin and Odin traditions of prophecy in Western and Northern Europe. But such madness always has very specific hallmarks, and forms only one part of a spiritual or prophetic cycle of maturity and inner realisation. It should never be taken out of its mythic or traditional context to mean simply that madness or wildness is always connected to prophecy, inspiration and poetry: this would clearly be nonsense, and even dangerous.

There are a number of ways that have always been acclaimed as routes to prophetic inspiration: all are rooted in ancient traditions, not simply because they derive from a past history or from what are often regarded as outmoded levels of religion and society, but because such traditions represent a distillation of human experience.

Different traditions express this distillation in different ways, and out of each tradition it permeates through the cultural symbols and collective mythology of any land, race, tribe, clan, or – to use a more technical definition – each transpersonal, temporally extended family. Modern magical orders, for example, which seem superficially to be very recently contrived and mainly literary entities, may truly trace certain of their roots back thousands of years. Such roots extend through specific imaginal contacts, techniques, and symbols that magical orders employ. This type of connection and continuity is what is implied by a transpersonal or temporally extended group or family.

The same extension of connective consciousness through tradition exists in certain castes or interlinked families and tribes of musicians, story tellers, bards, healers and, of course, of seers and prophets.

In this last context we find that there is a genetic aspect to seership, prophecy and inspiration: in Celtic lore the tradition asserts that seventh children (the seventh son or daughter), and, most potently, the seventh child of a seventh child, may have powers of spiritual healing and of prophetic inspiration. This genetic concept of seership is found worldwide, taking various traditional forms and roles according to the country in which it appears. To extend the genetic picture, certain religions such as Tibetan Buddhism also consider periods and signs of reincarnation. Very powerful spiritual beings reincarnate in certain genetic patterns, such as families, or specific lines of motherhood, or numerical generations, such as the seventh son of Celtic tradition mentioned above. There is an almost lost science of spiritual genetics by which it is possible firstly to define which individuals might have an inherent inner ability, such as prophecy, and secondly by which these persons might arouse their latent skill. But this is only an early stage, and later in spiritual disciplines the individual has to transcend and reabsorb his or her genetic inheritance, the latent or manifest genetic skills.

Rudolph Steiner, one of the few true modern seers, spiritual teachers, and prophets, described his experiences in which he had to set aside and finally re-attune his inherent magical or seership skills, for they were genetic, and therefore not part of humankind's fully expanded spiritual potential. Steiner is not stating anything new when he describes experiences and teachings of this sort: in medieval literature we find the same teaching applied to Lancelot of the Lake. He was the greatest warrior, the most skilled, the most daring, the most beautiful, with many advanced spiritual qualities. Yet all this was his inheritance, his genetic gift as we might put it in modern terms. Because he did not seek true spiritual growth but rather traded solely upon his innate skills, great as they were, he fell into spiritual perdition and eventual madness. This medieval allegory is merely a stylised version of an important teaching that deals with transpersonal growth and development. More simply we have to grow through effort and transmutation of our energies into new patterns: if we rely on inherent skills alone we ultimately consume ourselves and decay, rather than transform and enliven. This is yet another expression of the differences in octave between divination, seership, and prophecy that we have defined throughout this book.

4 · TECHNIQUES DEFINED

In most mystical magical and religious traditions we find not only the key concept of divine inspiration that cuts through all the trappings of religion and causes direct utterance of truth, but also some very specific techniques. Many of these techniques arise worldwide, while a smaller but significant number are unique to, and characteristic of, racial and environmental origins. If we were to select a shortlist, a primary set of such techniques for reference or for potential contemporary use, the following might be singled out for application within personal discipline, meditation, and contemplation.

FASTING AND PURIFICATION

This fundamental perennial mystical and magical practice need not be associated with concepts of 'holiness' or 'punishment for sins' or 'mortification of the flesh': such concepts are perversions of spiritual truth. The essentials of fasting and purification are very simple, and need not be taken to excess to have very noticeable results: indeed, excessive fasting and acts of purification may have a negative and imbalancing consequence. The main aim of fasting, bathing, induced sweating, and similar therapeutic acts is to cleanse the body, and particularly to cleanse the blood. The esoteric teaching concerning seership is that it involves a close relationship between the vital energies and the bloodstream.

If the body is full of toxins, unhealthy, overweight, attuned to self-gratification, it presents a potentially weak vehicle for prophetic energies. We frequently find that writers and teachers from the Christian era onwards assert that higher consciousness cannot be gained without purification, and that the physiological changes occasioned by fasting will inevitably lead to enhanced awareness. Conversely it is strongly asserted that those who fail to mortify the flesh will never attain to spiritual realisation, vision, insight, or illumination. All of this may be true for some individuals, but it would be more practical to use the simple analogy of the body as a vehicle: if it is sluggish and imbalanced it is endangered by an increased flow of energy: if it is fit and well tuned, it is better able to handle such forces.

CELIBACY OR ABSTINENCE FROM SEXUAL ACTIVITY

Here is another subject which, regrettably, has been perverted and corrupted by orthodox religion. It is perfectly clear, from historical and religious or mystical texts, that prophecy and spiritual development in general is not dependent upon sexual abstinence. Having said this much, which the reader may confirm for his or herself easily by further reading, celibacy or abstinence from sexual activity clearly plays an important role due its link to the orientation and flow of vital energies. The term abstinence is often misleading, for it actually implies control of the imagination, which may, when taken to extremes, be far more 'polluting' and unhealthy than harmonious regular sexual activity, which is, of course, a beneficial and spiritual affirmation of the powers of life.

A simple guideline might be to suggest that a period of abstinence will probably but not inevitably enhance seership or other inner abilities. It is up to the individual to undertake serious and carefully monitored experiments (which may be self-monitored through keeping a brief diary) over a period of at least one year, to gain any understanding of how the movement or stillness of sexual images and energies affects his or her consciousness. There are, however, advanced spiritual techniques within traditions in the East – such as Tantra which takes various forms in major Eastern religions and mystical or magical arts – where sexual polarity and exchange of energies between partners leads to intense and highly energised inner experiences.

TECHNIQUES OF MIND AND BODY

Both of the above categories are simply techniques applied to the mind and body through will and self-discipline. They are not essentially prophetic or spiritual in themselves. We must always remember that spiritual insight or inspiration comes, to use an old-fashioned phrase, willy-nilly (will-he or not-will-he), the spirit that bloweth where it listeth. This wild and unpredictable nature of spiritual inspiration is often overlooked, with commentators writing as if the techniques, training, traditions and symbolism were prophetic in themselves. They are, however, important and often valuable assets, for they give form and balance to wild power, to the inner fire, the prophetic breath, and enable it to work through an interface, a symbolic or mythic language that grants communication to a larger number of people.

The techniques of mind and body are also essential for the protection and rebalance of the seer, sybil or prophet: without them physical and mental illness frequently result from a sudden influx of higher consciousness or accelerated energies. We frequently find in modern literature the notion that the presence of higher forces or entities is assumed to be automatically beautiful and healing: this can indeed be the case, but only if the energies are channelled properly, and only if the individual is well prepared. The term channelled is used here in its proper sense, that of energies flowing through the body/psyche, and does not refer to mediumistic channelling such as is currently fashionable.

Techniques may usually include the following types of training:

1. BODY POSTURE AND POISE

The most refined expressions of this art are preserved in Eastern yoga traditions, but there are various Western postures that are often neglected or entirely unknown. These include the Hunter's posture (often inaccurately called the Buddha posture) of sitting cross-legged. We find this type of sitting and the related posture of squatting on the heels shown in ancient Celtic images of deities, and it is particularly used for balancing the body at rest while outdoors.

This position is frequently suggested as a meditational pose, from its ubiquitous presence in Eastern spiritual disciplines, but we find it in Western images more than two thousand years old, and therefore of an even more ancient origin, for the images were made during the Roman period, but based upon native non-Roman deities and religious traditions. One of the main cross-legged images is (with a number of examples known in Europe) of the Celtic divinity Cernunnos, lord of the animals and of subterranean wealth. This same deity is closely connected to the powers of prophecy, and in much later legends we find that Merlin becomes a wild man, keeper of animals, wearing horns, and involved with underworld powers[9].

Contrary to the rather prim suggestion frequently offered in primers on meditation that this posture isolates the meditator from the supposedly dull influence of earthly energies, it actually attunes the body and subtle energies to the Earth, for the genitals and their associated energy centres are close to the ground or touching it while seated in this posture. Furthermore, prophetic tradition frequently works through environmental and underworld forces, associated with the land and the planet, and there is no concept of airy disavowal of the sacred Earth.

A similarly important meditational posture from Hebrew or other Semitic traditions, which we know was used by the Old Testament prophets, was to sit with the head between the legs, with the body making a closed circle. This position is linked to the Kabbalistic Tree of Life, in which the human head is a lower octave of the universal Crown or source of all Being, Ultimate Divinity, while the human genitals and feet are lower octaves of the Foundation and Kingdom, the divine power and presence manifesting through into the material world. The greatest Kabbalistic mystery has always been that the Crown is inherent in the Kingdom, Spirit within Matter. Thus the meditational posture of placing the head between the legs close to the feet physically mirrors the fusion of the Crown and the Kingdom, making a circuit of vital energies.

In Christian iconography we see several important positions, such as the prayer position with palms together and hands raised, often accompanied by standing on tiptoe. Another, found worldwide, is the supplicant position, where the individual is balanced upon his or her knees, with arms opened wide. This is often connected to the tradition of *inflaming by prayer*, in which prayers or sacred verses are recited repeatedly, either aloud or inwardly, gradually causing a suspension of outer consciousness, and (hopefully) a contact with divinity.

2. MODES AND SYMBOLS OF AWARENESS

The body positions are generally linked to the use of specific imaginative symbols or images and clearly defined modes or levels of awareness, gained through training and constant practice. The most important of all of these is that of approaching Silence.

Modern sects, such as the Shakers and Quakers in Europe and America, developed an art of silent prayer, waiting for the spirit to move them to speak. This was nothing more nor less than a restatement in social form of the esoteric art of silent meditation, practised by religious and magical orders worldwide for millennia. Traditionally prophets prepared themselves for utterance by long periods of silent meditation, stilling all mentation, emotions, inner impulses, and so listening, and waiting, for the spiritual voice from deep within. Sometimes the voice seemed to come from above, or far away, while at other times it was uttered out of natural emblems, such as springs, trees, stars, or burning bushes. We shall return to this environmental aspect of prophecy shortly.

Other modes of awareness resonate outwards from relative stillness and silence: they include visionary experiences attuned to mythic and religious themes, previously defined states or degrees of apprehension and understanding, supported by symbols that are first taught in oral tradition or ritual training, and intense concentration upon chosen subject or objects. This last category is not merely mental weightlifting, but connects to the holistic nature of seership: by focusing upon one unit or expression, the seer or prophet may gain insight into greater harmonics, greater events, even into the universe itself.

INVOLVEMENT WITHIN A MYTHIC TRADITION

This is one of the most empowering means of gaining prophetic consciousness, and also provides the vehicle of translation for communicating the inspiration to other people. If we examine the various prophetic texts that have been preserved, it is clear that in most cases (excluding obvious frauds or political fabrications) the seer utters images and verses that partake of a mythic tradition, often highly conventionalised. Much of the apparent obscurity of early prophetic texts is nothing more nor less than the fact that modern readers, working at several linguistic removes and totally separated from the mythic traditions inherent within the text, cannot grasp items of cross reference or poetic convention that would have been commonplace to the speaker and his or her listeners or the author and readers of the original material.

Prophecy is intimately connected to Creation Myth, and many prophetic utterances are couched in terms of the story of the land and its inhabitants. We find, typically, that the presence of divinity, usually the tribal or environmental god or goddess, though often with a transcendent aspect, prepares the listener for statements concerning the future of the rulers, kingship being originally a sacred rather than a political role. This energy then permeates out through the land to affect everyone. Traditional prophecy is often harmonic or hierarchical: first the divine origin, then the power of king or queen mediating with the god or goddess, then other castes such as nobles, priesthoods, warriors, farmers and herders, and finally the ordinary or lower castes of folk. Usually prophecy is limited to the activities of leaders, for obvious reasons. Originally this prophetic role was due to the concept of divine power flowing out through the king or queen, priest or priestess, mediating transformative and regenerative forces to the land and the people. Later this becomes rationalised into a more political approach, for whatever the ruling classes do will affect the ordinary people. Eventually it becomes blatant politics, with a religious and occasionally prophetic structure set up to support the ruling classes. It is interesting to note, however, that prophecy gradually becomes suppressed or trivialised as politics gains power, particularly that pure prophecy of true spiritual utterance, which is often revolutionary and alarming to any status quo. We need not look only to modern materialist states for this change, but may find it clearly shown in the later Roman Empire, when trivial divination and prognostication ran riot, yet disturbing spiritual utterances were suppressed.

USE OF PHYSICAL AIDS TO SEERSHIP

There are a small number of physical aids to attaining prophetic consciousness: the secret of the art is always to stay with one specific system, immersed in a mythic and spiritual tradition. People who have rooms cluttered with crystal balls, Tarot cards, ouija boards, runes, pendulums, dowsing rods, oracular handbooks, pentacles and inscribed mirrors are usually frauds or superficial fiddlers.

If we consider the aids found in the works of genuine seers, sybils and prophets, we find that they inevitably stayed with one simple system. Nostradamus (see Chapter 7) used a bowl of water; the oracle at Delphi was inspired by vapour or steam; in the Merlin tradition certain key images appear, in the shape of humans, animals or otherworld beings. These later became formalised out of the old storytellers' repertoire into which they had devolved, to become the first Tarot cards.[10]

Many traditions use not only fasting and purification, but certain herbs or drugs. This is a difficult area to assess, as it is all too easily modernised into an excuse for trivial drug abuse, such as abounded in the 1960s when lysergic acid and cannabis oil were shrilly claimed to give cosmic insight and raise consciousness. What these drugs actually do is to break down the habitual filters or conditioned barrier of consciousness, erasing the parameters and orientation of perception. The illusion of a higher consciousness is soon dispelled when we realise that it is an illusion reliant upon a drug, and not a true property of willed changes of perception such as those obtained through the perennial spiritual disciplines. Such transformation cannot be bought, sold, smoked, imbibed or soaked into sugar lumps.

Having said all of the foregoing, there is no doubt that consciousness changing substances were frequently employed, sometimes regularly, and sometimes, as in initiatory rites, only once. With a regime of fasting and abstinence, ordinary and relatively harmless substances become highly potent, and the use of traditional plants, fungi and various combinations of substances is found worldwide. The higher art of prophecy, however, does not require drugs, but operates through the full individual entity without chemical aids: indeed, the arousal of the Inner Fire, or the Dragon Power, or *kundalini* makes distinct changes in the bloodstream. This is one of the so-called secrets of prophetic power, but it means nothing without the divine or transpersonal focus of awareness, and the return or response from higher worlds.

THE ENVIRONMENTAL CONNECTION

We have touched upon this aspect of prophecy in many places throughout this book, but it remains to discuss it as a major feature of the prophetic experience in its own right. Many prophets worked with or through the land, its inherent forces, its deities, and the myths of the people in the land. Having done so, however, they uttered truths from divinity, from the stars. Here is the connection between prophecy and mythic astrology or mythic astronomy. In this prophetic proto-astrology, we find that certain stellar patterns are considered of great importance. Often these are not the obvious risings of planets over the horizon or eclipses of the Moon or Sun, much beloved of rationalist writers who delight in asserting their superiority over the ignorant peoples of the unenlightened past, but directly observed seasonal variations that mark the ebb and flow of environmental and planetary lifetides.

The most distinctive of these are often assumed to be the solar solstices and equinoxes, and their variable correlation to the solar system planets, and to phases of the Moon: a typical example might be that of solar equinox synchronised with a full Moon or conversely with a dark Moon. The Lunar phase will directly modify and modulate the deeper effect of the solar threshold of the Equinox. Prophets sought inspiration by meditation in sacred locations, often while looking at the visible patterns of the stars and planets in association with the Sun and Moon. Once the pattern had been observed, the seer meditated in the open within, as it was said, the influence of the subtle rays and forces of the stellar or planetary relationship.

A close relationship between the Moon and Venus implied forces connected to sexuality, love, life energies, and fertility. A similar relationship between the Moon and Mars related to war, the fall or rise of rulers and kings, and so forth. This type of astrology is not necessarily worked through calculation, but through a relatively small number of traditional attributes being used as a basis for contemplation and meditation. Such meditations were usually carried out in locations that were, in themselves, power centres, sacred nodes of geomantic or racial energy. This is a far cry indeed from our modern astrology with computers, and our modern ley-line enthusiasts with their plastic-handled dowsing wires and other apparatus. The human being, therefore, acted as a *mediator*, a connecting link, between the upper and lower worlds.

There is, unfortunately, a habitual tendency for modern writers and revivalists, drawing mainly from Victorian or Edwardian sources, boldly to assert that solar seasons and lunar or planetary appearances steered the calendar of the ancient world. Entire mythic structures and sagas, philosophies and religions are reduced to merely seasonal rotations or agricultural cycles. The truth is often simpler yet more perplexing and profound.

In fact we find that a small number of minor stellar groupings, or certain constellations hardly mentioned in modern works on astrology, mythology or magical arts, play very important roles indeed. In the case of the Pleiades, for example, a tradition exists extending around our whole world. When this tiny group of stars appears or disappears over the horizon (in early May and November) races in both the Northern and Southern hemispheres use them as markers for the thresholds of the year: May marks the beginning of summer, November the beginning of winter. Yet we are repeatedly and inaccurately informed by writers who have failed to check their facts that the great May and November festivals of the Celts, the Scandinavians, the Greeks, the South American civilisations, the natives of New Guinea and Pacific cultures, were to celebrate or induce the death and rebirth of the Sun.

Furthermore the Pleiades play a major role in esoteric and prophetic traditions: many primal peoples, even today, assert that their ancestors travelled from the Pleiades to the Earth. This is no mere science-fiction plot, but a living tradition connected to a small group of stars that might hardly seem to merit such attention, yet act as the markers of the world, all over our planet, in many ancient civilisations and modern but primal cultures.[11]

The human seer mediated forces from above and below: prophecy is intimately connected to the land and to the hidden and often dark forces of the underworld. We find that the inspiration for the sybil at Delphi was said to be a mysterious breath emanating from a fissure in the Earth: the oracle itself was originally dedicated to the Great Mother; its totem animal was the snake, and even the dominant role of Apollo barely masks the underworld powers of the shrine and its oracular practices. Indeed, Apollo is a variable god, connected both to the Underworld and to the Sun.

In Celtic tradition all life and death energies, all mysterious forces of creation and dissolution, were found in the Underworld. This was a major feature of pagan Celtic religion, and in the later traditions associated with Merlin as prophet, we find many underworld attributes. The most famous is, of course, his utterance of prophecies reaching to the end of the solar system, which arose while underground in the presence of two dragons (see pp 95–97). This is the legendary reference to a tradition of a fusion of the Earth forces and the vital energies of the human seer, both of which were represented as dragons. The technique involves methods by which the vital energies within one's own body/consciousness are set into resonance with those of the geomantic location: many oracles and oracular practices were operated literally underground.

In Aquae Sulis (Bath, England) an ancient oracular shrine of the Celts dedicated to the goddess Sul or Sulis, whose name means eye, *gap, orifice*, was greatly expanded and rebuilt by the conquering Romans from the first to the fourth centuries. Sul, who was a rather dark goddess concerned with cursing, childbirth and prophecy, was amalgamated with the more staid Roman Minerva, who herself was a variant of the Greek Athena, and related to the Celtic goddess of poetic inspiration, Brigh or Brigit, to whom an eternal flame was dedicated[12].

It is significant that archaeologists have found evidence that the Romans built an artificial chamber over the copious hot spring that formed the sacred locus to the temple complex. This was enclosed, as if to resemble a cave, and a pier or walkway was built out to provide a platform in the middle of the rising steam. Presumably, though there is no factual evidence, this was where the sybil sat to utter prophecies, inspired (as at Delphi) by the god or goddess issuing a mysterious breath or vapour from the depths below.

5 · THE BEGINNING AND THE END:
CREATION AND APOCALYPSE

Prophecy, and specific prophecies, cannot be separated from a cultural tradition, from the people and the land in which they originated.

Prophecy is nothing more nor less than part of the mythic Story of All ... the prophet is able, through perception of universal or stellar forces, to tell certain parts of the creation story that are not yet known to others.

It is easy to spend time and effort in discussing aspects or modes of consciousness and the defining energies of prophecy, as if these occurred in a vacuum devoid of any other symbolic or imaginative language. This is, of course, untrue, for prophecy and indeed specific prophecies, cannot be separated from a cultural tradition, from the people and the land in which they originated. This may seem rather obvious, a simple historical or sociological truth; but there are some subtle and potent ramifications to this simple fact, connected to creation mythology, and the development of human culture and human relationship to the land and the planet – to the environment.

Ultimately the environment is not the green field next door about to be turned into a nuclear power station, nor even the land or continent: it is our entire world, our solar system, and enfolding that solar system is the world of the stellar universe.

This seems rather grand, even mystically pretentious, but there can be little doubt that ancient mythology and religion fused the environmental and the stellar, seeing no difference between the two, other than the essential difference of proportions, or of octaves. To grasp this simple but elusive fact we may examine so-called hard evidence, such as archaeology, revealing that ancient temples and worship sites were frequently aligned to stellar patterns, mirroring the universe upon the surface of the Earth through patterns and proportions. We might read ancient literature, ranging from religious texts to philosophical treatises, and find hidden or overtly stated that the stellar and planetary forces and entities play a major role in the energies and events upon Earth. We could then resort to modern physics, which has developed an integrated holistic model of the universe, where energies and events are consubstantial and interpenetrate one another. Modern materialist science is now proving mystical truths by a roundabout route, through two centuries of gross reductionism and misery that have brought us to the brink of planetary suicide.

But we need not, if we so choose, apply to any of the foregoing, for there is ample evidence from world mythology. Creation myths begin in the void, in chaos, in the primal condition from which Being utters itself subsequently to resonate or proliferate as various worlds, dimensions, realities, and their occupants.

The mythic process is essentially harmonic, one of reflections and polarities. Its interactions expand and contract through myriad worlds and beings, eventually leading to the generation of our Solar System, and our primal Earth. This is then populated with orders of life, plants, birds and animals, humans, and other natural and supernatural creatures, this last category travelling between zones or worlds more freely than humanity. From this point in mythology – a very late stage in the creation process, – human history (as mythic history) begins. And in this earliest of mythic proto-historical phases, we find the earliest sources of prophecy. Prophecy is nothing more nor less than part of the mythic Story of All: the prophet is able, through perception of universal or stellar forces, to tell certain parts of the creation story that are not yet known to others.

We now come to an essential feature of prophecy, the tradition of apocalyptic vision. Prophecy in general is a very specific aspect of Creation Myth, but working only through exalted or transcendent levels of consciousness, rather than the recitation or retelling of preserved lore. The imagery of prophecy therefore combines elements from creation mythology with both religious and chaotic or sometimes heretical and sacrilegious material. Prophetic visions often retain or perhaps regenerate symbols and mythic aspects of religion and magic that predate whatever orthodox state religious structure exists in the prophet's culture.

A number of mythic cycles preserve stories concerning the end of the world: sometimes they refer to previous world orders that have been destroyed and rebuilt in a new form: the creation story, therefore, at the beginning of the mythic cycle often includes a destruction tale. This early destruction may mirror the promised ending of the world or apocalypse, or it may be upon a defined level that is to be replaced totally by a new level of destruction in an age yet to come. Thus in Hindu mythology we find that there are vast cycles of birth and death for the universe, with many world-ages calculated and the powers of destruction and creation extensively defined. Simpler versions are preserved in Semitic mythology permeating religions such as Judaism, or Christianity. The Christian destructive imagery begins with water, the Flood, but promises Fire for the end of the current world order. This progression is not unusual, for it represents a universal cycle of the Elements, each world age ending through the agency of one particular Element.

Prophetic vision is often concerned with the Elements and with universal octaves or transcendent powers which are the Elements as aspects of ultimate Being, the relative phases of the holism or pleroma of existence.

The presence of chaotic imagery in prophecy often derives from mythic cycles preserved as formal verses or in many cases as diffuse tales, using their vocabulary and symbols in a manner that represents the heightened consciousness and the vision of the seer. But in addition to using mythic or religious vocabularies, prophets sometimes attempt to describe what they perceive in its own paradoxical condition, seeking to reveal the vision, the entities, the forces, in dramatic and startling terms that will galvanise the listener or reader into some new level of perception. Thus we have a number of highly individual texts preserved from various cultures, in which we find orthodox imagery and terminology fused with highly unorthodox visions.

In some texts, however, we find quite the opposite concept, for the esoteric heart of the prophecy is hidden deliberately in obscure terminology, often requiring oral instruction or specific initiation into the school of symbolism within which the prophet originally trained. Descriptions of transcendent states, worlds, dimensions, entities and so forth are, in this context, preserved and passed on to aid the student, offering signposts in the difficult exploration of the inner or metaphysical realms. Thus the thirteenth-century vision of Thomas Rhymer (see Appendix I) preserves an ancient Celtic mythology, guiding the listener or trainee seer through the realms of the Underworld and of the Sidh or Fairy people. It is both the vision and journey that Thomas experienced, according to tradition, and a map by which those who seek to follow him may be guided. After his visionary experience he was able to make accurate prophecies. Specific visions are often used in this manner, and there is much to be gained by employing them on modern visualisation and meditation.

EXAMPLES OF APOCALYPTIC TEXTS

Primal apocalyptic texts are found in mythic cycles: in Greek mythology we encounter the destruction theme in the unending war between the Titans and the Olympians; in Norse mythology a similar polarity is found, in which the primal ice and fire giants and vast universal destructive monsters will eventually destroy the Three Worlds and consume the Moon, Sun and Stars.

The apocalyptic content of Christianity derives from older Jewish texts, albeit adapted and often carefully selected and edited. Nevertheless, it is in the apocalyptic visions, such as that of Revelation, that we find truly ancient lore breaking through into the new religion.

CHAPTER 6

And I saw when the Lamb opened one of the seven seals, and I heard one of the four living creatures saying as with a voice of thunder, Come.

2. And I saw, and behold, a white horse, and he that sat thereon had a bow; and there was given unto him a crown: and he came forth conquering, and to conquer.

3. And when he opened the second seal, I heard the second living creature saying, Come.

4. And another horse came forth, a red horse: and to him that sat thereon it was given to take peace from the earth, and that they should slay one another: and there was given unto him a great sword.

5. And when he opened the third seal, I heard the third living creature saying, Come. And I saw, and behold, a black horse; and he that sat thereon had a balance in his hand.

6. And I heard as it were a voice in the midst of the four living creatures saying, A measure of wheat for a penny and three measures of barley for a penny; and the oil and the wine hurt thou not.

7. And when he opened the fourth seal, I heard the voice of the fourth living creature saying, Come.

8. And I saw, and behold, a pale horse: and he that sat upon him, his name was Death; and Hades followed with him. And there was given unto them authority over the fourth part of the earth, to kill with sword, and with famine, and with death, and by the wild beasts of the earth.

9. And when he opened the fifth seal, I saw underneath the altar the souls of them that had been slain for the word of God, and for the testimony which they held:

10. And they cried with a great voice, saying, How long, O Master, the holy and true, dost thou not judge and avenge our blood on them that dwell on the earth?

11. And there was given them to each one a white robe; and it was said unto them, that they should rest yet for a little time, until their fellow-servants also and their brethren, which should be killed even as they were, should be fulfilled.

12. And I saw when he opened the sixth seal, and there was a great earthquake; and the sun became black as sackcloth of hair, and the whole moon became as blood;

13. And the stars of the heaven fell unto the earth, as a fig tree casteth her unripe figs, when she is shaken of a great wind.

14. And the heaven was removed as a scroll when it is rolled up; and every mountain and island were moved out of their places.

15. And the kings of the earth, and the princes, and the chief captains, and the rich, and the strong, and every bondman and

freeman, hid themselves in the caves and in the rocks of the mountains;

16. And they say to the mountains and to the rocks, Fall on us, and hide us from the face of him that sitteth on the throne, and from the wrath of the Lamb:

17. For the great day of their wrath is come; and who is able to stand?

CHAPTER 8

And when he opened the seventh seal, there followed a silence in heaven about the space of half an hour.

2. And I saw the seven angels which stand before God; and there were given unto them seven trumpets.

3. And another angel came and stood over the altar, having a golden censer; and there was given unto him much incense, that he should add it unto the prayers of all the saints upon the golden altar which was before the throne.

4. And the smoke of the incense, with the prayers of the saints, went up before God out of the angel's hand.

5. And the angel taketh the censer; and he filled it with the fire of the altar, and cast it upon the earth: and there followed thunders, and voices, and lightnings, and an earthquake.

6. And the seven angels which had the seven trumpets prepared themselves to sound.

7. And the first sounded, and there followed hail and fire, mingled with blood, and they were cast upon the earth: and the third part of the earth was burnt up, and the third part of the trees was burnt up, and all green grass was burnt up.

8. And the second angel sounded, and as it were a great mountain burning with fire was cast into the sea: and the third part of the sea became blood;

9. And there died the third part of the creatures which were in the sea, even they that had life; and the third part of the ships was destroyed.

10. And the third angel sounded, and there fell from heaven a great star, burning as a torch, and it fell upon the third part of the rivers, and upon the fountains of the waters;

11. And the name of the star is called Wormwood: and the third part of the waters became wormwood; and many men died of the waters, because they were made bitter.

12. And the fourth angel sounded, and the third part of the sun was smitten, and the third part of the moon, and the third part of the stars; that the third part of them should be darkened, and the day should not shine for the third part of it, and the night in like manner.

13. And I saw, and I heard an eagle, flying in mid heaven, saying with a great voice, Woe, woe, woe, for them that dwell on the earth, by reason of the other voices of the trumpet of the three angels, who are yet to sound.

CHAPTER 9

And the fifth angel sounded, and I saw a star from heaven fallen unto the earth: and there was given to him the key of the pit of the abyss.

2. And he opened the pit of the abyss; and there went up a smoke out of the pit, as the smoke of a great furnace; and the sun and the air were darkened by reason of the smoke of the pit.

3. And out of the smoke came forth locusts upon the earth; and power was given them, as the scorpions of the earth have power.

4. And it was said unto them that they should not hurt the grass of the earth, neither any green thing, neither any tree, but only such men as have not the seal of God on their foreheads.

5. And it was given them that they should not kill them, but that they should be tormented five months: and their torment was as the torment of a scorpion, when it striketh a man.

6. And in those days men shall seek death, and shall in no wise find it; and they shall desire to die, and death fleeth from them.

7. And the shapes of the locusts were like unto horses prepared for war; and upon their heads as it were crowns like unto gold, and their faces were as men's faces.

8. And they had hair as the hair of women, and their teeth were as *the teeth* of lions.

9. And they had breastplates, as it were breastplates of iron; and the sound of their wings was as the sound of chariots, of many horses rushing to war.

10. And they have tails like unto scorpions, and stings; and in their tails is their power to hurt men five months.

11. They have over them as king the angel of the abyss: his name in Hebrew is Abaddon, and in the Greek *tongue* he hath the name Apollyon.

12. The first Woe is past: behold, there come yet two Woes hereafter.

13. And the sixth angel sounded, and I heard a voice from the horns of the golden altar which is before God,

14. One saying to the sixth angel, which had the trumpet, Loose the four angels which are bound at the great river Euphrates.

15. And the four angels were loosed, which had been prepared for the hour and day and month and year, that they should kill the third part of men.

16. And the number of the armies of the horsemen was twice ten thousand times ten thousand: I heard the number of them.

17. And thus I saw the horses in the vision, and them that sat on them, having breastplates *as* of fire and of hyacinth and of brimstone: and the heads of the horses are as the heads of lions; and out of their mouths proceedeth fire and smoke and brimstone.

18. By these three plagues was the third part of men killed, by the fire and the smoke and the brimstone, which proceeded out of their mouths.

19. For the power of the horses is in their mouth, and in their tails: for their tails are like unto serpents, and have heads; and with them they do hurt.

20. And the rest of mankind, which were not killed with these plagues, repented not of the works of their hands, that they should not worship devils, and the idols of gold, and of silver, and of brass, and of stone, and of wood; which can neither see, nor hear, nor walk:

21. And they repented not of their murders, nor of their sorceries, nor of their fornication, nor of their thefts.

Similar imagery is found in the older text The Book of Enoch, which is likely to have been familiar to the writer of The Book of Revelation. Enoch, one of the greatest Hebrew prophets, is said to have vanished corporeally: Enoch walked with God and was not. A mystical tradition, often asserted in Kabbalistic teachings, and curiously finding its way in medieval Grail lore, states that Enoch, once a human prophet, became the great Archangel next to the Throne of God.[13] In the Book of Enoch, we find a progression through various houses or states of spiritual perception and entity:

Behold the clouds invited me and mist summoned me, and the course of the stars and the lightnings sped and hastened me, and the winds in the vision caused me to fly and lifted me upward, and bore me into heaven. And I went in till I drew nigh unto a wall which is built of crystal and surrounded by tongues of fire, and it began to make me afraid. And I went into the tongues of fire and drew nigh to a large house which was built of crystals, and the walls of that house were like a tessellated floor made of crystal and its groundwork was of crystal

(Enoch xiv: 8–10).

It has occasionally been suggested that experiences of this sort, appearing in medieval literature such as the Merlin texts, the Grail texts, and the vision of Thomas Rhymer, are simply stylised copies of Christian, Judaic or earlier books known to monastic scholars. This is, of course, propagandist nonsense. All prophetic visions draw upon a core tradition of imagery and guided journeys through the otherworld: we find it in classical, Celtic, Norse, and Semitic mythology, in orthodox religious texts, and then find parallels worldwide in every culture, religion or country. Typically the apocalyse or visions of cosmic destruction are of a stellar nature: just as creation begins beyond and before the stars in the chaotic void, so is the ultimate drawing in of existence a stellar matter, and not limited to the purging or redemption of the planet Earth or the human world alone.

In Enoch xviii: 12–16 we find a typical examples of such imagery, fusing the concept of chaos and negative dimensions or zones, a concept which was later to provide such terrible potential for suppressive dogma in political Christianity.

There I saw a place which had no firmament of the heaven above, and no firmly founded earth beneath it: there was no water upon it, and no birds, but it was a waste and horrible place. I saw there seven stars like great burning mountains, and when I enquired regarding them the angel said: This place is the end of heaven and earth: this place has become a prison for the stars and the host of heaven. The stars which roll over the fire are those which have transgressed the commandment of the Lord in the beginning or their rising, because they did not come forth at their appointed time. And he was wroth with them and bound them till the time when their guilt should be consummated, even for ten thousand years.

In the medieval *Prophecies of Merlin* we find a detailed apocalyptic vision, which one would perhaps expect to draw substantially upon the Book of Revelation, especially as the writer, Geoffrey of Monmouth, was in the higher orders of the Catholic Church, as a member of the Norman aristocracy of the period. Instead we find that Geoffrey has preserved an ancient Celtic tradition, probably rewriting oral verses declaimed to him by a Welsh or Breton bard and storyteller, the traditional verses ascribed to Merlin. Here the apocalypse seems to be partly derived from Greek astrology, and partly from a fusion of the Celtic and classical cosmologies. Direct Biblical references and tone are absent, though there are some parallels.

Root and branch shall change place and the newness of the thing shall pass as a miracle. The brightness of the Sun shall fade at the amber of Mercury, and horror shall seize the beholders. Stilbon of Arcadia shall change his shield: the Helmet of Mars shall call Venus.

The Helmet of Mars shall make shadow, and the rage of Mercury shall exceed his orbit. Iron Orion shall unsheathe his sword; the marine Phoebus shall torment the clouds. Jupiter shall go out of his lawful paths; and Venus forsake her appointed circuits.

The malignity of the star Saturn shall slay mankind with a crooked sickle. The Twelve Houses of the Stars shall lament the irregular excursions of their inmates.

The Gemini shall omit their usual embrace, and will call Aquarius to the fountains. The Scales of Libra shall hang awry, till Aries puts his crooked horns under them. The tail of Scorpio shall produce lightning, and Cancer quarrel with the Sun. Virgo shall mount upon the back of Sagittarius, and darken her Virgin flowers [i.e. lose her virginity].

The Chariot of the Moon shall disorder the Zodiac, and the Pleiades shall break forth into weeping. No offices of Janus shall return hereafter, but his gate being shut shall lie hidden in the depths of Ariadne.

The seas shall rise up in the twinkling of an eye, and the dust of the Ancients be restored. The [four] winds shall fight together with a dreadful blast, and their Sound shall reach to the Stars.

(R. J. Stewart, From *The Prophetic Vision of Merlin* Penguin, Arkana (1986 and 1989). The verses quoted are based upon the translation by J. G. Giles (1896).)

This rather daunting vision is one of those that requires inside knowledge, for it fuses several symbolic structures and traditions.

Most specifically it involves that type of prophetic astrology which we refer to on page 36, astrology of a quite different kind to the modern calculations and rigid patterns that are used today. In this vision, the seer has seen the breakdown of the order's solar system, with special emphasis upon the role of Orion and the Pleiades. These were both significant stellar entities in the ancient world, but play no part at all in modern astrology.

A number of parallels to Merlin's apocalypse may be suggested, but none seems to act as a direct source, for this was in the oral bardic material which Geoffrey of Monmouth reassembled into Latin. In the *Pharsalia* of Lucan (Book I) a seer, Figulus, consults the omens for the outcome of the war between Caesar and Pompey: he states that either mankind is headed for ultimate ruin, or the stars have broken the boundaries of their natural laws. The imagery is similar to that of the Merlin text, and we know that Geoffrey was familiar with Lucan's *Pharsalia* and *History*, for he quotes them elsewhere. Some elements of the cosmology, therefore, may derive from classical influence, and particularly that of the Stoic philosophers.

Another popular prophetic text, well known in the Middle Ages, is the *Oracula Sybillina*, dating from the first century AD. This text was widespread in Europe, a version being found as far north as Iceland. Biblical parallels to the Merlin apocalypse are to be found in Revelation vi: 13; xii: 4; Isaiah xiii: 10. We may make an enlightening comparison with Mark xiii: 24–27:

> But in those days after that tribulation, the sun shall be darkened, and the moon shall not give her light, and the stars shall be falling from heaven, and the powers that are in the heavens shall be shaken. And then shall he send forth the angels, and shall gather together his elect from the four winds, from the uttermost part of the earth to the uttermost part of heaven.

Here we find the apocalypse, the solar or cosmic dissolution, but none of the ancient astrology, and no stellar entities such as Orion or the Pleiades. The fourfold pattern, however, of the Four Winds is used to show the elect being summoned by angels. In the Merlin texts there is no presence whatsoever of a redeemer or an elect, and this is perhaps the most significant evidence that they are indeed ancient prophetic verses predating Christianity, though many further proofs could be cited.

In Isaiah we find the stellar imagery incorporated into a typical prophetic warning and cursing of the sinful Children of Israel:

'For the stars of heaven and the constellations thereof shall not give their light: the sun shall be darkened in his going forth, and the moon shall not cause her light to shine.' It seems likely that there was a general store of stellar mythic imagery found in the ancient world, and that fragments of this lore appear in different visions and apocalypses, according to the culture or tradition concerned. The fundamental themes are those of stellar disorientation, the breaking of the world order, and the ending of a cycle of creation. The imagery may be used poetically, as it seems to be in Isaiah where the bulk of the text concerns the punishment of the Lord's people, and clearly is not a cosmic vision. In Mark, however, we seem to be in the presence of prediction and promise of salvation for the elect when the cosmic dissolution occurs. The Book of Revelation, of course, abounds in such imagery.

There are other parallels in non-canonical apocalyptic visions from Jewish tradition, and in Kabbalistic mysticism. Norse myth, as we have mentioned briefly, contains some extensive visions of *Ragnarok*, the chaotic destruction of the worlds by primal monstrous beings. There may be some relationship between Norse, Greek, Celtic and Middle Eastern myth, particularly in terms of mystical or metaphysical expansions and initiators teachings, which all include concepts such as the multiple worlds, the Tree of Life and orders of being linking the worlds together, and the Creation and Destruction cycles.

6 · THE POWER OF PROPHECY

There are a number of detailed descriptions of the experience of prophecy found in ancient and subsequent texts from the medieval period onwards. The classical theory of prophecy, as defined in the ancient world, was twofold. Firstly the individual could be raised to an exalted or transpersonal state of consciousness: this is the definition of pure prophecy which is used throughout this book. The second source of prophecy, widespread in the pagan world, and still found in primal magical arts today in isolated cultures, was that an entirely different and highly potent entity would displace the ego or individuality of the seer, and speak through his or her mouth. Occasionally the two sources might be fused, for an elevation of consciousness into higher modes or worlds might lead to the insertion of a spiritual entity into the physical organism of the seer for purposes of prophetic declaration.

The second process, that of displacement or control, seems at first glance to be similar to that of the spiritualist medium of the nineteenth and twentieth centuries. But if we examine sources in detail, we find quite a different story. The invasion or displacement of the human individual's ego or personality by a divine entity was, in the ancient world, a terrible and terrifying experience, very different indeed from the rather comfortable and reassuring style of modern mediumship in which a medium has his or her spirit guide who temporarily assumes control but essentially takes care of the human partner.

We need only turn to one of the most famous texts of the classical world, Virgil's *Aeneid*, to find a detailed description of the oracle of Apollo, working by displacement through the Sybil of Cumae. Her persona or ego is tortured by the irresistible and terrible force of Phoebus Apollo, which she attempts unsuccessfully to resist. Although we should make some allowances for Virgil's poetic licence and dramatic style, the description is based directly upon the oracular methods of the classical world, and has many parallels worldwide. A similar displacement is described in the twentieth century in the Tibetan state oracle, where the medium was male. Many primitive societies use displacement for prophecy, and we find it especially active in modern voodoo cults. In the Sixth Book of the Aeneid we find this passage, describing the oracle, and the effect of the power of Apollo upon the sybil:

A vast cavern is scooped in the side of the Euboîc cliff, whither lead an hundred wide passages by an hundred gates, whence peal forth as manifold the responses of the Sibyl. They had reached the threshold, when the maiden cries: 'It is time to enquire thy fate: the god, lo! the god.' And even as she spoke thus in the gateway, suddenly countenance nor colour nor ranged tresses stayed the same; her wild heart heaves madly in her panting bosom; and she expands to sight, and her voice is more than mortal, now the god breathes on her in nearer deity. 'Lingerest thou to vow and pray,' she cries, 'Aeneas of Troy? lingerest thou? for not till then will the vast portals of the spellbound house swing open.' So spoke she, and sank to silence. A cold shiver ran through the Teucrians' iron frames, and the king pours heart-deep supplication:

'Phoebus, who hast ever pitied the sore travail of Troy, who didst guide the Dardanian shaft from Paris' hand full on the son of Aeacus, in thy leading have I pierced all these seas that skirt mighty lands, the Massylian nations far withdrawn, and fields that the Syrtes fringe; now at last we catch at the flying skirts of Italy; thus far let the fortune of Troy follow us. You too may now unforbidden spare the nation of Pergama, gods and goddesses to whomsoever Ilium and the great glory of Dardania did wrong. And thou, O prophetess most holy, foreknower of the future, grant (for no unearned realm does my destiny claim) a resting-place in Latium to the Teucrians, to their wandering gods and the storm-tossed deities of Troy. Then will I ordain to

Phoebus a temple of solid marble, and festal days in Phoebus' name. Thee likewise a mighty sanctuary awaits in our realm. For here will I place thine oracles and the secrets of destiny uttered to my people and consecrate chosen men, O gracious one. Only commit not thou thy verses to leaves, lest they fly disordered, the sport of rushing winds; thyself utter them, I beseech thee.' His lips made an end of utterance.

But the prophetess, not yet tame to Phoebus' hand, rages fiercely in the cavern, so she may shake the mighty godhead from her breast; so much the more does he tire her maddened mouth and subdue her wild breast and shape her to his pressure. And now the hundred mighty portals of the house open of their own accord, and bring through the air the answer of the soothsayer:

'O thou for whom the great perils of the sea are at last over, though heavier yet by land await thee, the Dardanians shall come to the realm of Lavinium; relieve thy heart of this care; but not so shall they have joy of their coming. Wars, grim wars I discern, and Tiber afoam with streams of blood. A Simoïs shall not fail thee, a Xanthus, a Dorian camp; another Achilles is already provided in Latium, he too goddess-born; nor shall Juno's presence ever leave the Teucrians; while thou in thy need, to what nations or what towns of Italy shalt thou not sue! Again is an alien bride the source of all that Teucrian woe, again a foreign marriage-chamber . . . . Yield not thou to distresses, but all the bolder go forth to meet them, as thy fortune shall allow thee way. The path of rescue, little as thou deemest it, shall first open from a Grecian town.'

In such words the Sibyl of Cumae chants from the shrine her perplexing terrors, echoing through the cavern truth wrapped in obscurity: so does Apollo clash the reins and ply the goad in her maddened breast. So soon as the spasm ceased and the raving lips sank to silence, Aeneas the hero begins: 'No shape of toil, O maiden, rise strange or sudden on my sight; all this ere now have I guessed and inly rehearsed in spirit. One thing I pray; since here is the gate named of the infernal king, and the darkling marsh of Acheron's overflow, be it given me to go to my beloved father, to see him face to face; teach thou the way, and open the consecrated portals.

(J.W. Mackail (trans), 1885)

There is, however, another method of communion between higher entities and humanity, which has attracted much attention in recent years in esoteric arts, and which has become known as *mediation*.

This is a harmonic process, where the consciousness and energy of a higher entity is attuned through that of the human mediator: the essential difference between this process and that of either the spiritualist medium or the paroxysm of the sybil is that the mediator remains in full individual consciousness. Mediation is one of the skilled arts of ritual magic and of spiritual technology which is to be found in the rituals of world religion. Such techniques cause spiritual or higher forces to flow through the mediator, priest of priestess, without ever passing into utterance of trance of prophetic frenzy. The spiritual art of mediation, therefore, is not a prophetic one, though it can under some circumstances lead to empowered statements or utterances by or through the mediator. In orthodox religion, at any rate, mediation is firmly contained by the shape and text of the liturgy: in private or magical spiritual arts, the mediation is, again, usually carefully defined.[14]

7 · NOSTRADAMUS

Nostradamus is perhaps the most famous prophet, excepting those at the heart of orthodox religion. He was born in Provence in 1503, and died in 1566. He was a renowned doctor of medicine, an astrologer, and an initiate of the mystical and magical arts. That he could survive at all is something of a miracle, in an age of intense religious persecution, yet his prophecies commanded enormous attention during and immediately after his lifetime, and have run through many translations and editions from the sixteenth to the twentieth century.

So much nonsense has been written about Nostradamus, particularly in the context of interpretation of his prophetic verse, that it is difficult to assess briefly the value of his work. The key to such an evaluation lies not in correlating individual predictions, fascinating though this may be, but in the philosophical, metaphysical and practical notes that he left for future generations. Prophecy taken out of context is valueless: we cannot truly understand the Hebrew prophets without their religion, their culture, nor can we understand the divinatory arts of the ancients without such a background. To truly grasp the importance of the Prophecies of Merlin, which are in the same tradition as the works of Nostradamus, though earlier by at least four centuries, we must delve into Celtic and ancient Greek magical arts, astrology, and prophetic traditions. If we take any of these examples, and many more might be cited, and simply quote a few tantalising verses and suggest clever interpretations, we totally destroy the deeper spirit of the prophecy.

Though many editions of Nostradamus' verses exist in modern interpretations, his contribution to the art of prophecy is not limited to specific examples. If we examine his descriptions of prophetic art, which some commentators have described as 'obscure' or 'confusing', we find that he clearly restates the classical art of divination and prophecy in Renaissance terms, limiting himself strictly to the techniques and effects that a practitioner might experience. He represents, therefore, an enduring tradition, that appears through various historical eras. This is not the Biblical or Semitic tradition, nor is it that of the oracle of possession or mediumship. It relates rather to the ancient prophetic-astrology, in which the seer is filled with a divine vision that has stellar resonances or counterparts.

At the opening of his *Centuries* Nostradamus follows the hallowed tradition by which a description of the method of prophecy prefaces the actual results. We find this in a number of such texts, and our examples include those of Merlin and Thomas Rhymer, both of whom, like Nostradamus, have had false prophecies added to their names in various publications.

The technique used by Nostradamus has been known since classical times, and is found in Iamblichus' *De Mysteriis Egyptorum*, quoted on pp.44–45. As an edition of this fourth century text was published in 1547, it probably influenced Nostradamus, though we must not discount an oral initiation, or indeed the influence of a number of other possible classical or mystical texts. The first two verses of his first *Century* (a book of one hundred verses) describe the use of a tripod, upon which the prophet sits, or possibly of a *scrying* bowl, which was filled with water and set upon the tripod to act as a focus of attention. Similar methods have been used for thousands of years, and were widespread in both folk custom and secret formalised magical arts. Not far away in Elizabethan England Doctor John Dee (1527–1608) was communicating with the spirit world by means of scrying in a *shew-stone* or crystal. He was less concerned with prophecy, however, than with an entire science and language of inter-dimensional knowledge, much of which was to influence later occultists and magicians.

> *Estant assis de nuict secret estude*
> *Seul reposé sur la selle d'aerian;*
> *Flambe exiguë sortant de solitude*
> *Fait prosperer qui n'est à croire vain.*
> *La verge en main mise au milieu des* BRANCHES

De l'onde il moulle (et) le limbe (et) le pied
Un peur (et) voix frémissant par les manches;
Splendeur divine. Le divin près s'assied
(from the Rigaud edition, 1568).

Being seated at night in a secret study, concentrating solely upon the brass tripod [or possibly: alone upon the aery stool]. A slender flame issues from emptiness, making to prosper that which is not to be believed in vainly [or possibly: bringing out *who* is not to be vainly believed in].

The rod in the hand is placed in the middle of the BRANCHES,
With the wave [water] he moistens the border [hem] and the foot.
A moment of fear and a voice, trembling in the sleeves:
Splendour divine. The god sits close.

(R. J. Stewart, transl.)

Nostradamus uses the phrase '*flambe exiguë sortant de solitude*' which perfectly describes the light or fire or spiritual inspiration issuing from silence, an experience frequently asserted by seers, mystics, and magicians. There is a ritual element to his operations, for he uses a wand, and lustrates or purifies himself with the dedicated water. Then a voice is heard, causing him to tremble with fear. A very specific phrase is used to describe the next stage of the ritual: *Splendeur divine. Le divin près s'assied.*' Splendour divine: the god sits close.

This is nothing more nor less than a compressed description of a pagan prophetic experience. In the original text there is a codified reference in capitals, BRANCHES. This refers to the legs of the stool or tripod, but also would have directed the classically educated reader towards the oracular techniques of the pythoness of Apollo, and the Oracle of Branchus. Nostradamus is not, however, taken over by the god (not God, but the god: *le divin*, for the god sits close in divine splendour.)

The text has that typical condensed multifold layering of meaning found in other oracular and magical verses, and this persists throughout the prophecies which follow. Interpretation is by no means as easy as has often been suggested, though there is no doubt that many of the verses, rightly or wrongly interpreted, had a profound effect upon European princes and politicians, even into the twentieth century.

Another curious connection that springs to mind is with the language of Dr Dee's *Hieroglyphic Monad*, a mystical text of approximately the same period. Dee's short, profound book deals, on one of its many levels of meaning, with what is nowadays called the *circulation of light* or the sexual energies that amplify and transform consciousness.

Now the text of the *Centuries* begins to expound specific prophecies, many of which are incomprehensible, some of which seems to have come true. But for further insights into the prophetic method, we can hardly improve upon Nostradamus own description, written for his infant son.

PRÉFACE À MON FILS
THE PREFACE OF MICHAEL NOSTRADAMUS TO HIS PROPHECIES

To Caesar Nostradamus his son, life and felicity. Thy late arrival, Caesar Nostradamus my son, has made me bestow much time, through nightly vigils, to leave you in writing a memorial to refer to, after the corporal extinction of your progenitor, that might serve for the common profit of mankind, out of what the Divine Being has permitted me to learn from the revolution of the stars. And since it has pleased the immortal God that thou shouldst come into the natural light of this terrene abode, and shouldst say that thy years are not yet calculated astronomically, and thy March months are incapable to receive in their weak understanding what I must necessarily record as to happen after my time: – seeing also that it is not possible to leave thee in writing what might suffer injury and be obliterated by time; for the inherited gift of occult prediction will remain confined to my own bowels: – considering that events of human proposal are uncertain, while all is governed and directed by the incalculable power of Heaven, guiding us, not by Bacchic fury, nor yet by Lympathic motion, but by astronomical assertion – '*Soli numine divino afflati præsagiunt et spirito prophetico particularia.*' ['Such alone as are inspired by the divine power can predict particular events in a spirit of prophecy.']

Although for years past I have predicted, a long time in advance, what has afterwards come to pass, and in particular regions attributing the whole accomplishment to divine power and inspiration, also other unfortunate and fortunate occurrences have been pronounced with accelerated promptitude which have since happened in other parts of the world – for I was willing to maintain silence and to pass over matters that might prove injurious if published not only as relates to the present time, but also for the most part of future time, if committed to writing, since kingdoms, sects, and religions will pass through stages so very contrary, and, as regards the present time, diametrically opposed – that if I were to relate what will happen in the future, governors, sectaries, and ecclesiastics would find it so ill-accordant with their auricular fancy, that they would go near to condemn what future ages will know and perceive to be true. Considering also the sentence of the true Saviour, '*Nolite sanctum dare canibus neque mittatis margaritas vestras ante porcos, ne forte conculcent eas pedibus suis, et conversi dirumpant vos*' [Matt. vii. 6].

This it is which has led me to withold my tongue from the vulgar, and my pen from paper. But, later on, I thought I would enlarge a little, and declare in dark and abstruse sayings in consideration of the vulgar advent the most urgent of its future causes, as perceived by me, be the revolutionary changes what they may, so only as not to scandalize the auricular frigidity (of my hearers), and write all down under a cloudy figure that shall essentially and above all things be prophetical. Although '*Abscondidisti hoec à sapientibus, et prudentibus, id est, potentibus, et regibus, et enucleasti ea exiguis et tenuibus.*' ['Thou hast hidden these things from the wise and prudent, *i.e.*, from the powerful and from kings, and hast revealed them to the small and weak.' This is Nostradamus's gloss upon Matt. xi. 25.] By the grace of God and the good angels, the Prophets have had committed to them the spirit of vaticination, by which they see things at a distance, and are enabled to forecast future events. For there is nothing that can be accomplished without Him, whose power and goodness are so great to all His creatures as long as they put their trust in Him, much as they may be exposed or subject to other influences, yet on account of their likeness to the nature of their good guardian angel that heat and prophetic power draweth nigh to us, as do the rays of the sun which cast their influence alike upon bodies that are elementary and non-elementary. As for ourselves personally who are but human, we can attain to nothing by our own unaided natural knowledge, nor the bent of our intelligence, in the way of deciphering the recondite secrets of God the Creator. '*Quia non est nostrum noscere tempora, nec momenta,*' Acts i. 7. Although, indeed, now or herafter some persons may arrive to whom God Almighty may be pleased to reveal by imaginative impression some secrets of the future, as accorded in time past to judicial astrology, when a certain power and volitional faculty came upon them, as a flame of fire appears. They grew inspired, and were able to judge of all inspiration, human and divine, alike. For the divine works, which are absolutely universal, God will complete; those which are contingent, or medial, the good angels direct; and the third sort come under the evil angels.

Perhaps, my son, I speak to thee here a little too occultly. But as to the hidden vaticinations which come to one by the subtle spirit of fire, or sometimes by the understanding disturbed, contemplating the remotest stars, as being intelligences on the watch, even to giving utterance to declarations being taken down in writing declare, without favour, and without any taint of improper loquacity, that all things whatsoever proceed from the divine power of the great eternal Deity from whom all goodness emanates. Further, my son, although I have inserted the name of prophet, I do not desire to assume a title of so high sublimity at the present moment. For he who 'Propheta dicitur hodie, olim vocabatur videns', ['He who is called prophet now, once was called seer,'] for, strictly speaking, my son, a prophet is one who sees things remote from the knowledge of all mankind. Or, to put the case; to the prophet, by means of the perfect light of prophecy, there lie opened up very manifestly divine things as well as human; which cannot come about, seeing that the effects of future prediction extend to such remote periods. Now, the secrets of God are incomprehensible, and their efficient virtue belongs to a sphere far remote from natural knowledge; for, deriving their immediate origin from the free will, things set in motion causes that of themselves could never attract such attention as could make them recognized, either by human augury, or by any other knowledge of occult power; it is a thing comprised only within the concavity of heaven itself, from the present fact of all eternity, which comes in itself to embrace all time.

Still, by the means of some eternal power, by an epileptic Herculean agitation, the causes by the celestial movement became known. I do not say, my son, in order that you may fully understand me, that the knowledge of this matter cannot yet impress itself upon thy feeble brain, that very remote future causes may not come within the cognizance of a reasonable being; if they are, notwithstanding, purely the creation of the intellectual soul of things present, future things are not by any means too hidden or concealed. But the perfect knowledge of causes cannot be acquired without divine inspiration; since all prophetic inspiration derives its first motive principle from God the Creator, next from good fortune, and then from nature. Wherefore the independent causes being independently produced, or not produced, the presage partially happens, where it was predicted. For the human understanding, being intellectually created, cannot penetrate occult causes, otherwise than by the voice of a genius by means of the thin flame showing to what direction future causes incline to develop themselves. And further, my son, I implore you never to apply your understanding on such reveries and vanities as dry up the body and bring perdition to the soul and disturb all the senses. In like manner, I caution you against the seduction of a more than execrable magic, that has been denounced already by the sacred Scriptures, by the divine canons of the Church – although we have to exempt from this judgement Judicial Astrology. By the aid of this it is, and by divine revelation and inspiration, united with deep calculations, we have reduced our prophecies to writing. And, notwithstanding that this occult philosophy was not reproved by the Church, I have felt no desire to divulge their unbridled promptings. Although many volumes have come before me, which had laid hidden for many ages. But dreading what might happen in the future, after reading them, I presented them to Vulcan, and as the fire kindled them, the flame, licking the air, shot forth an unaccustomed brightness, clearer than the light is of natural flame, resembling more the explosion of powder, casting a subtle illumination over the house as if the whole were wrapped in sudden conflagration. – So that at last you might not in the future be abused by searching for the perfect transformation, lunar or solar, or incorruptible metals hidden under the earth, or the sea, I reduced them to ashes. – But as to the judgement which perfects itself by means of the celestial judgement, that I am desirous to manifest to you: by that method you may have cognizance of things future, avoiding all fantastic imaginations that may arise, and limiting the particularity of the topics by divine and supernatural inspiration; harmonizing with the celestial figures these topics, and that part of time, which the occult property has relation to, by the potential virtue and faculty divine, in whose presence the three aspects of times are clasped in one by eternity – an evolution that connects in one causes past, present, and future – 'quia omnia sunt nuda et aperta', ['For all things are naked and open.']

From all which, my son, you can easily comprehend, notwithstanding your tender brain, the things that are to happen can be foretold by nocturnal and celestial lights, which are natural, coupled to a spirit of prophecy – not that I would assume the name or efficacy of a prophet, but, by revealed inspiration, as a mortal man the senses place me no farther from heaven than the feet are from the earth. '*Possum non errare, falli, decipi*,' albeit I am the greatest sinner in this world, and heir to every human affliction. But being surprised sometimes in the ecstatic work, amid prolonged calculation, and engaged in nocturnal studies of sweet odour, I have composed books of prophecies, containing each one hundred astronomic quatrains of forecasts, which I have tried to polish through obscurely, and which are perpetual vaticinations, from now to the year 3797. It is possible that this figure will make some lift up their forehead, at such a vast extent of time, and variety of things to take place under the concave journey of the moon; and this universal treatment of causes, my son, throughout the earth, which, if you reach the natural age of man, you will see in your climate, under the heaven of your proper nativity, as things that have been foreseen.

Although the everlasting God alone knows the eternity of the light proceeding from Himself, I say frankly to all to whom He has decreed in long and melancholy inspiration to reveal His limitless magnitude, which is beyond both mensuration and comprehension, that by means of this occult cause divinely manifested, principally by two chief causes, comprised in the understanding of the inspired one who prophesies. One is that which comes by infusion, which clarifies the supernatural light, in him who predicts by astral process, or forecasts by inspired revelation, which is practically a participation in the divine eternity, by which means the prophet comes to judge of that which his share of divine spirit has given him, by means of communication with God the Creator, and the natural endowment accorded him. It is to know that what is predicted is true, and has had a heavenly origin; that such light and the thin flame is altogether efficacious; that it descends from above, no less than does natural clearness; and natural light renders philosophers quite sure of their principles, so that by means of the principles of a first cause they have penetrated the profoundest abysses and attained the loftiest doctrines.

But to this end, my son, that I may not wander too profoundly for the future capacity of thy senses, and also because I find that letters shall suffer great and incomparable loss, and that I find the world before the universal conflagration, such deluges and deep submersion, that there will remain scarcely any land not covered with water, and that for so long a period, that everything will perish except Ethnographies and Topographies. Further, after and before these inundations, in many districts the rains will have been so slight, and there will fall from heaven such an abundance of fire and incandescent stones, that scarcely anything will remain unconsumed, and this will occur a short time before the last conflagration. Further, when the planet Mars completes its cycle, at the end of this second period, he will recommence his course. But some will gather in Aquarius through several years, and others in Cancer, which will be of still longer duration. Now that we are conducted by the moon, under the direction of the Creator, and before she has finished her entire circuit the sun will come, and then Saturn. Now, according to the celestial signs, the reign of Saturn shall come back again, so that, all calculated, the world is drawing on towards its anaragonic revolution.

From the time I was writing this, before 177 years 3 months and 11 days, by pestilence, long famine, and wars, and more still by inundations, the world between this day and that, before and after, shall be diminished, and its population so reduced that there will hardly be hands enough to attend to agriculture, and the lands will be left as long without culture as they have been under tillage. This, so far as celestial judgement manifests, that we are now in the seventh millenary, which completes all and introduces us to the eighth, where is the upper firmament of the eighth sphere, which, in a latitudinary dimension, is where the Almighty will come to complete the revolution, where the celestial figures will return to their courses, and the upper motion which renders the earth stable for us and fixed, 'non inclinabitur in seculum seculorum,' ['Whence it shall not deviate from age to age,'] unless His will be accomplished, and not otherwise.

Although by ambiguous opinions exceeding all natural reason by Mahometical dreams, also sometimes God the Creator by the ministry of angels of fire, and missive flame, presents to the external senses, even of our eyes, the causes of future predictions, that indicate the future event which must manifest itself to him who presages anything. For the presage which is made by the exterior light comes infallibly to judge partly with and by means of the exterior flame; although truly the part which seems to come by the eye of the understanding springs only from the lesion of the imaginative sense. The reason is too evident, the whole is predicted by the afflatus of divinity, and by means of the angelic spirit inspired to the man prophesying, rendering him anointed with vaticinations, visiting him to illuminate him, and, stirring the forefront of his phantasy by divers nightly apparitions no less than daily certitude, he prophesies by astronomic administration conjoined with the holiest future prediction, taking nothing into his consideration but the hardihood of his free courage.

Come at this hour to understand, my son, that I find by my revelations, and which are in accordance with revealed inspiration, that the sword of death is on its way to us now, in the shape of pestilence, war (more horrible than has been known for three generations of men), and famine, that shall fall upon the earth, and return upon it at frequent intervals. For the stars accord with such a revolution, and with the written word, '*Visitabo in virgâ ferrea iniquitates eorum, et in verberibus percutiam eos.*' ['I will visit their iniquities with a rod of iron, and with blows will strike them.'] For the mercy of God, my son, will not be spread abroad for a time, till the major part of my prophecies shall have been accomplished, and have become by accomplishment resolved. Thus oftentimes in the course of these sinister storms the Lord will say, '*Conteram ego, et confringam, et non miserebor.*'[1] And a thousand other accidents will come by waters and continual rain, as I have more fully and at large set forth in my other Prophecies, which are drawn out at length, *in solutâ oratione*; (in these I) designate the localities, times, and terms prefixed, that all men who come after may see, recognizing the circumstances that come about by infallible indications. As we have marked by the others where we speak more clearly, for although they are covered with a veil of cloud, they are clear enough to be comprehended by men of good intelligence: '*Sed quando submoventa erit ignorantia*,' the total will stand out with greater clearance still. Making an end here, my son, take now this gift of thy father, Michael Nostradamus, hoping to expound to thee each several prophecy of these quatrains here given, beseeching the immortal Father that He will endue thee with a long life of happy and prospering felicity.

From Salon, this 1st of March, 1555.

8 · THE PROPHECIES OF MERLIN

In the middle of the twelfth century Geoffrey of Monmouth, a member of the Norman-based ruling class and a churchman, began to assemble the legendary history and other matter of ancient Britain. The result was a major book, the *History of the Kings of Britain*, and a few years later a masterly verse biography of Merlin, *The Vita Merlini*: both books were written in Latin, this being the international learned language of the period, though both contain elements of old Welsh or Breton (the 'British' language) and Greek, and even a small number of Arabic and Hebrew terms and motifs, so wide was Geoffrey's learning and so international were the contacts of the court and Church of the period.

Both the *History* and the *Vita* contain an enormous amount of Celtic lore, intermingled with classical sources, and fused with the general education available to a learned man of the day. There seems little doubt that Geoffrey noted the extensive oral traditions, and possibly had access to some already written material, deriving from bardic tradition. Geoffrey himself says that he copied the material from a great book in the British tongue, but this really seems to be a conventional apology, typical to many writers of the medieval period. The great book was, of course, not a material manuscript, but the collective source of history and tradition.

In Geoffrey's day there was a very active oral tradition of mythic history, genealogy, prophecy, heroic poetry and similar matters, circulated by travelling story-tellers, poets, and the specialised class known in Wales and Brittany as Bards. These bards were a remnant of the old Druidic castes from the pagan Celtic culture of the pre-Roman period, which persisted in various forms through the Roman period, and into the early Christian period. The Druids are supposed to have been divided into three castes: bards, vates (prophets), and druids (judges). Those castes or orders correspond to the Three Worlds and the Three Wheels (see Figure 1).

By the twelfth century, however, the lore of the Druids was extinct as a formal religion, but still active in Wales, Brittany, Ireland and Scotland on the level of folklore and communal knowledge or oral tradition and collective ritual and superstition. As late as the sixteenth century an Elizabethan spy reported back from north Wales, stating that the people there held large, illicit gatherings on mountainsides, at which they recited genealogies of princes and poetry and prophecies of Merlin and Taliesin; Taliesin being, like Merlin, a major figure in Welsh Celtic lore and legend.

Much of Geoffrey's source material derives, in terms of its content and style, if not from an actual early text, linguistically and culturally from a Welsh or Breton source, presumably a bard or bards. Geoffrey himself may have been partly Welsh or Breton. In the twelfth century the language of much of Wales and of Brittany was virtually identical, as there had been a steady cultural exchange between the two regions for several centuries, and many Welsh Britons seem to have emigrated to Brittany from approximately the fifth century onwards.[15]

In early chronicles we find it repeatedly asserted that this was a mass emigration to avoid the influx of Saxons arriving from the fifth century onwards from the east of England and of course, originally, from Europe. The actual pattern of emigration and exchange seems to have been more gradual and diffuse, and to have been coloured by the later chroniclers such as Gildas into a dramatic racial conflict.

Modern archaeologists are now beginning to suggest that there was considerable interchange between the Britons or Celts and Saxons during this important transitional period. In the context of Merlin, who is essentially a Welsh and Scottish prophet, with traditions found in north Wales and lowland to midland Scotland (but not, incidentally, anywhere in England), we might ponder upon his relationship to the Scandinavian god Odin, with whom he shares certain attributes.

There is no suggestion here, however, that Merlin is anything but a Celtic figure, probably dating back to antiquity as a god-form, and later appearing as title or name for specific prophets inspired by known images and working within well-defined traditional parameters, many of which are clearly stated in Geoffrey's books. The mythic links between Merlin, Odin, Apollo and other entities in the collective stream of magical and prophetic arts have been discussed elsewhere.[16]

It was Geoffrey's work that, almost single-handed, started the vast flood of Arthurian literature that was soon to follow, for before his books there was very little on Arthur, but after the dissemination of the *History of the Kings of Britain* a veritable explosion of Arthurian texts occurred, in Latin, Norman French, even in English. And along with this developed the extensive mystical and heretical Grail lore and literature, drawing upon a fusion of Celtic sources with certain hidden traditions perpetuated in some of the medieval monasteries, where such texts were generally, though not exclusively, assembled or written.

Set in the middle of the *History of the Kings of Britain* is an enigmatic – some would say fantastic – text, quite different in content and style from the remainder of the book. This text, a separate two-volume book in its own right, inserted at a dramatic point in the mythic history, consists of the *Prophecies of Merlin*.

As has been suggested in several of our chapters, prophecy and creation myth are closely linked together. We find this quite clearly expressed in Geoffrey of Monmouth's *History*, which is a vast tapestry of mythic history, legend, actual history, and stylish literary creation. In its very heart are the two books of the Prophecies, the first of which reiterates many of the events found in the main historical text, but then leaps far ahead to describe British future history, with some continental connections. The second book deals with deeper metaphysical matters in the main, though it too touches upon British future history, reaching (according to my own interpretation)[17] into the twenty-first century. The apocalypse comes shortly after the twenty-first century, in which the end of the Solar System is described. This section of the *Prophecies of Merlin* is found in Chapter 5, where apocalyptic prophecies are discussed.

Whatever the origins of Geoffrey's literary material, he describes clearly the prophetic inspiration or fit. Merlin is not a wise elder at this stage in his life, but still a youth. The usurping king Vortigern seeks to sacrifice him to uphold a tottering tower through evil magical arts. Merlin reveals that under the tower is a cave, and in the cave a pool, and in the pool two dragons lie sleeping.

Vortigern and Merlin descend into the cave and the pool is drained, whereupon the dragons issue forth. Merlin *bursts into tears*, one of the classic signs of prophetic consciousness breaking through and affecting the body. He then utters the Prophecies themselves. The method, though couched in an allegorical tale, is well described. A fusion of energies from beneath the Earth, symbolised by the cavern, pool, and dragons, arouses the prophetic power within the young Merlin. The dragons are both an environmental or, as they are described in the *History*, a racial energy, which has its counterpart in the individual. This is known variously as the Inner Fire, the power of *kundalini* (in Hindu terminology) or the serpent or dragon power. It is an esoteric aspect of the vital energies, and often linked to sexual energies, hence the traditional emphasis on sexual abstinence or purification of the imagination (see pp.58–63).

SELECTED PROPHECIES OF MERLIN

The Prophecies reach from the time of Vortigern, for whom a dismal end is correctly predicted, well into the twentieth and twenty-first century. Perhaps the most interesting to consider in a short survey of prophecy in general are those which seem to apply to the present era. A long line of kings and events is declared, and the nineteenth and twentieth centuries seem to be heralded with the verse:

> All these things shall Three Ages see, till the buried Kings shall be exposed to public view in the city of London.

We might take this to mean that the burials in Westminster Abbey become a tourist attraction. The Three Ages defined in the Prophecies are:
1. 6th–11th centuries, from the Saxon to the Norman period;
2. 11th–17th centuries, marked by prophecies predicting the united crown which only appeared with the accession of James I of England who was also James VIth of Scotland;
3. 17–21st centuries, including a number of prophecies that seems very apt to the present day and the immediate future.

> In those days the oaks of the forest shall burn, and acorns grow upon lime trees The Severn Sea shall discharge itself through seven mouths, and the river Usk burn for seven months. Fishes shall die in the heat thereof, and from them serpents will be born.

At present the Severn Estuary (Sea) is the site of nuclear power stations, and it is only too easy to feel that this verse represents some terrible environmental disaster in this context. Since I first examined the Prophecies in the late 1970s, a massive tidal barrage has been designed for the Severn, which would literally discharge its waters through multiple mouths, to turn turbines.

> The baths of Badon [Bath, England] shall grow cold, and their health giving waters shall engender death/London shall mourn for the death of twenty thousand, and the river Thames shall be turned to blood. The monks in their cowls shall be forced to marry, and their cry shall be heard upon the mountains for the Alps.

Between 1979 and 1981 the health-giving hot springs of Bath, site of the famous prophetic temples of Sulis Minerva, dating from the Romano-Celtic period of the first to fourth centuries, were declared polluted. Bathing was banned, and the public were not admitted to the spring, as it was found to contain amoeba, which were said to be the cause of death in a young woman. Despite that fact that such amoeba are found in hot springs all over the world, and the likelihood of infection is millions to one, it does seem that this event reflects the prophecy accurately.

More recently a reader has suggested to me that the lines regarding death and the forced marriage of monastics may be a garbled prediction of the appearance of the Aids virus, which is mainly transmitted sexually. I reserve judgement on this matter.

> The River Thames shall encompass London, and the fame of this work shall pass beyond the Alps./The Hedgehog shall hoard his apples within it, and shall make subterranean passages./At that time shall the stones speak, and the area towards the Gallic coast be contracted into a narrow space./On each bank shall one man hear another, and the soil of the island shall be enlarged./The secrets of the deep shall be revealed, and Gaul shall tremble for fear.

Present-day London is prevented from being encompassed by the Thames by a complex tidal-barrier scheme, without which the city would flood. The hedgehog is a symbol of wealth, due to the allegory of the wealthy man being like a hedgehog who rolled in apples and came up with them stuck upon his bristles. London is a world centre of commerce and wealth, and is now permeated by a complicated underground tunnels system, carrying trains, sewers, electricity, water, and all the services of the present century.

We certainly have speaking stones, for our entire microchip technology works through such wonders: and a man standing on the shore of Britain can indeed talk directly to a man standing on the shore of France (Gaul), by means of telephone, radio, satellite television and many other devices enabled by speaking stones. A tunnel is being made to bring Britain and France much closer together by rail. We might indeed think that this set of images applies to the late twentieth century.

MAGICAL OR TRANSFORMATIONAL IMAGES

Like many prophetic texts or vision, the *Prophecies of Merlin* provide some detailed information and imagery concerning their origin. In this case we find images of loosely disguised Celtic or other pagan deities, and particularly an important image of the Goddess of the Land, known in Irish tradition as Sovereignty. It is clear, both from the Prophecies and from many other sources, that the Goddess of the Land was the enabling power that presided over kings, prophets, and poets. In Ireland and Scotland the popularised Saint Bride or Brigit is a variant of the pagan goddess Brig. She was a goddess of fire and light, smithcraft (metal working and jewellery) of therapy, and of poetic inspiration – the fire within the breast. This same goddess was found in various ancient temples in differing forms, of which Athena, Minerva, and Vesta are typical examples.

Shortly before the modern history, quoted above, and the apocalypse (quoted on page 76) we find a sequence describing the goddess of the land, who appears out of the ancient forest as a maiden, purifies three rivers, and grows to maturity. The rivers are described as those of Life, Hunger (Desire), and Death, the most ancient triplicity sacred to the Great Goddess.

Once she has practised her oracular arts, she shall dry up the noxious fountains by breathing upon them Afterwards she shall refresh herself with the [transformed] wholesome liquor, and she shall carry in her right hand the forests of Caledonia and in her left the buttressed walls of London.

Thus the goddess unites the land, from the far north (the forests of Caledonia or Scotland) to the civilised south (the buttressed walls of London). She purifies the fountains, practises oracular arts, and unifies the land. This is the power behind the prophets, bards and seers, of the Celtic tradition.

Figure 3   Psychic and Spiritual Transformation and levels of consciousness in the Vita Merlini

SYMBOLIC AND TOTEM ANIMALS

Many prophetic texts or utterances use animal imagery in a number of different forms: some animals are employed to represent people, a simple (though sometimes infuriatingly difficult) set of blinds which might only be understood by a contemporary person.

In other contexts animals are magical images: they represent forces or energies which the prophet perceives, and to which he or she portrays as animals that embody those forces or qualities.

99

Thus the Lion represents courage, and is also a solar symbol. The Eagle represents kingship, flight, vision. The Salmon in Western and Northern Europe represents wisdom; the Serpent represents underworld energies, and so forth.

In the Prophecies there are many animal images, used for varying purposes. Sometimes they are powerful symbols, while at others they clearly represent actual historical or future-historical persons. In the *Vita Merlini* we find the traditional wisdom of animal lore linked to the holistic concept of a total universe, in which everything from cosmic forces, stars, planetary winds and weather and all living beings, interact with one another. Long lists of creatures are given, and some of them elate to magical and prophetic powers or abilities. Merlin spends a period of his life in madness, living in the forest, and acting as Lord of the Animals an ancient pagan image embodied by both Pan and the Celtic Cernunnos. At this level we have a very deep-rooted link between the transformative arts and energies of magic and prophecy, and the embodiment of such energies in life forms, including their presence within human consciousness. The psychic and spiritual transformation and levels of consciousness in the *Vita Merlini* are shown in Figure 3.

To conclude this short survey of prophecy in the Merlin tradition, here is one of the most complex, difficult and obscure passages: it is full of strange animals of all sorts.

51A. After these things shall come forth a heron from the forest of Calaterium, which shall fly round the island for two years together. With her nocturnal cry she shall call together the winged kind, and assemble to her all sorts of fowls. They shall invade the tillage of husbandmen, and devour all the grain of the harvests. 52. Then shall follow a famine upon the people, and a grievous mortality upon the famine. But when this calamity shall be over, a detestable bird shall go to the valley of Galabes, and shall raise it to be a high mountain. Upon the top thereof it shall also plant an oak, and build its nest in its branches. Three eggs shall be produced in the nest, from whence shall come forth a fox, a wolf, and a bear. 53. The fox shall devour her mother, and bear the head of an ass. In this monstrous form shall she frighten her brothers, and make them fly into Neustria. But they shall stir up the tusky boar, and returning in a fleet shall encounter with the fox; who at the beginning of the fight shall feign herself dead, and move the boar to compassion. 54. Then shall the boar approach her carcass, and standing over her, shall breathe upon her face and eyes. But she, not forgetting her cunning, shall bite his left foot, and pluck it off from his body. Then shall she leap upon him, and snatch away his right ear and tail, and hide herself in the caverns of the mountains. 55. Therefore shall the deluded boar require the wolf and bear to restore him his members; who, as soon as they shall enter into the cause, shall promise two feet of the fox, together with the ear and tail, and of these they shall make up the members of a hog. 56. With this he shall be satisfied, and expect the promised restitution. In the meantime shall the fox descend from the mountains, and change herself into a wolf, and under pretence of holding a conference with the boar, she shall go to him, and craftily devour him. 57. After that she shall transform herself into a boar, and feigning a loss of some members, shall wait for her brothers; but as soon as they are come, she shall suddenly kill them with her tusks, and shall be crowned with the head of a lion. 58. In her days shall a serpent be brought forth, which shall be a destroyer of mankind. With its length it shall encompass London, and devour all that pass by it. 59. The mountain ox shall take the head of a wolf, and whiten his teeth in the Severn. He shall gather to him the flocks of Albania and Cambria, which shall drink the river Thames dry. 60. The ass shall call the goat with the long beard, and shall borrow his shape. Therefore shall the mountain ox be incensed, and having called the wolf, shall become a horned bull against them. In the exercise of his cruelty he shall devour their flesh and bones, but shall be burned upon the top of Urian. 61. The ashes of his funeral-pile shall be turned into swans, that shall swim on dry ground as on a river. They shall devour fishes in fishes, and swallow up men in men. 62. But when old age shall come upon them, they shall become sea-wolves, and practise their frauds in the deep. They shall drown ships, and collect no small quantity of silver. 63. The Thames shall again flow, and assembling together the rivers, shall pass beyond the bounds of its channel. It shall cover the adjacent cities, and overturn the mountains that oppose its course. 64. Being full of deceit and wickedness, it shall make use of the fountain Galabes. Hence shall arise factions provoking the Venedotians to war. The oaks of the forest shall meet together, and encounter the rocks of the Gewisseans. 65. A raven shall attend with the kites, and devour the carcasses of the slain. An owl shall build her nest upon the walls of Gloucester, and in her nest shall be brought forth an ass. 66. The serpent of

Malvernia shall bring him up, and put him upon many fraudulent practices. Having taken the crown, he shall ascend on high, and frighten the people of the country with his hideous braying. 67. In his days shall the Pachaian mountains tremble, and the provinces be deprived of their woods. For there shall come a worm with a fiery breath, and with the vapour it sends forth shall burn up the trees. Out of it shall proceed seven lions deformed with the heads of goats. With the stench of their nostrils they shall corrupt women, and make wives turn common prostitutes. 68. The father shall not know his own son, because they shall grow wanton like brute beasts. Then shall come the giant of wickedness, and terrify all with the sharpness of his eyes. Against him shall arise the dragon of Worcester, and shall endeavour to banish him. 69. But in the engagement the dragon shall be worsted, and oppressed by the wickedness of the conqueror. For he shall mount upon the dragon, and putting off his garment shall sit upon him naked. The dragon shall bear him up on high, and beat his naked rider with his tail erected. Upon this the giant rousing up his whole strength, shall break his jaws with his sword. At last the dragon shall fold itself up under its tail, and die of poison. 70. After him shall succeed the boar of Totness, and oppress the people with grievous tyranny. Gloucester shall send forth a lion, and shall disturb him in his cruelty, in several battles. He shall trample him under his feet, and terrify him with open jaws. 71. At last the lion shall quarrel with the kingdom, and get upon the backs of the nobility. A bull shall come into the quarrel, and strike the lion with his right foot. He shall drive him through all the inns in the kingdom, but shall break his horns against the walls of Oxford. 72. The fox of Kaerdubalem shall take revenge on the lion, and destroy him entirely with her teeth. She shall be encompassed by the adder of Lincoln, who with a horrible hiss shall give notice of his presence to a multitude of dragons. 73. Then shall the dragons encounter, and tear one another to pieces. The winged shall oppress that which wants wings, and fasten its claws into the poisonous cheeks. Others shall come into the quarrel, and kill one another. 74. A fifth shall succeed those that are slain, and by various stratagems shall destroy the rest. He shall get upon the back of one with his sword, and sever his head from his body. Then throwing off his garment, he shall get upon another, and put his right and left hand upon his tail. Thus being naked shall he overcome him, whom when clothed he was not able to deal with. 75. The rest

he shall gall in their flight, and drive them round the kingdom.
Upon this shall come a roaring lion dreadful for his monstrous
cruelty. Fifteen parts shall he reduce to one, and shall alone
possess the people. 76. The giant of the snow-white colour shall
shine, and cause the white people to flourish. Pleasures shall
effeminate the princes, and they shall suddenly be changed into
beasts. 77. Among them shall arise a lion swelled with human
gore. Under him shall a reaper be placed in the standing corn,
who, while he is reaping, shall be oppressed by him. A charioteer
of York shall appease them, and having banished his lord, shall
mount upon the chariot which he shall drive. With his sword
unsheathed shall he threaten the East, and fill the tracks of his
wheels with blood. 78. Afterwards he shall become a sea-fish,
who, being roused up with the hissing of a serpent, shall engender
with him. From hence shall be produced three thundering bulls,
who having eaten up their pastures shall be turned into trees.
The first shall carry a whip of vipers, and turn his back upon
the next. 79. He shall endeavour to snatch away the whip, but
shall be taken by the last. They shall turn away their faces from
one another, till they have thrown away the poisoned cup. 80.
To him shall succeed a husbandman of Albania, at whose back
shall be a serpent. He shall be employed in ploughing the ground,
that the country may become white with corn. The serpent shall
endeavour to diffuse his poison, in order to blast the harvest.
81. A grievous mortality shall sweep away the people, and the
walls of cities shall be made desolate. There shall be given for a
remedy the city of Claudius, which shall interpose the nurse of
the scourger. For she shall bear a dose of medicine, and in a short
time the island shall be restored. 82. Then shall two successively
sway the sceptre, whom a horned dragon shall serve. One shall
come in armour, and shall ride upon a flying serpent. He shall
sit upon his back with his naked body, and cast his right hand
upon his tail. With his cry shall the seas be moved, and he shall
strike terror into the second. 83. The second therefore shall enter
into confederacy with the lion; but a quarrel happening, they shall
encounter one another. They shall distress one another, but the
courage of the beast shall gain the advantage. 84. Then shall come
one with a drum, and appease the rage of the lion. Therefore shall
the people of the kingdom be at peace, and provoke the lion to a
dose of physic. In his established seat he shall adjust the weights,
but shall stretch out his hands into Albania. For which reason
the northern provinces shall be grieved, and open the gates of

the temples. 85. The sign-bearing wolf shall lead his troops, and surround Cornwall with his tail. He shall be opposed by a soldier in a chariot, who shall transform that people into a boar. The boar shall therefore ravage the provinces, but shall hide his head in the depth of Severn. 86. A man shall embrace a lion in wine, and the dazzling brightness of gold shall blind the eyes of beholders. Silver shall whiten in the circumference, and torment several wine presses. Men shall be drunk with wine, and regardless of heaven, shall be intent upon the earth. 87. From them shall the Stars turn away their faces and confound their usual course. Corn will wither at their malign aspects, and there shall fall no dew from Heaven.

9 · PROPHECY AND PROPAGANDA

When we consider later European prophecies, we find them to be similar in many ways to those of the classical world, but with some unique characteristics which derive from native religion or wisdom traditions such as those of the Celtic or Scandinavian cultures. As we might expect they often take a Christian tone, but surprisingly this does not always derive from the basic orthodoxy of the Church. Prophecy, even when presented by members of the religious hierarchy, always smacked of paganism or heresy. We shall return to this uneasy relationship between prophecy and formal religion shortly.

The best-known examples of later European prophecy are those of Nostradamus (see pp.83–92 and Appendix III) dating from the sixteenth century, but there are many more that have not come to the attention of modern fashion. Due to the strong Christian rule and influence we find that prophecy took two main directions from the early medieval period, and both remain in existence in an attenuated form even today. The two branches were also present in classical prophecy, and undoubtedly formed part of the prophetic traditions of Eastern cultures such as those of the Egyptians, Babylonians, and Jews, but the division between them tends to be highlighted in medieval and later Europe due to the ascendancy of political Christianity.

The first branch is, superficially if not actually, connected to the Apocalyptic Vision, though in many cases the apocalypse within the prophecies themselves is clearly non-Christian and highly unorthodox. These are usually known as millenarianist or millennial prophecies. They subdivide into two further branches, those which are entirely political, using the cloak of prophecy to loosely disguise what would nowadays be called revolutionary propaganda, and those with a genuine prophetic or apocalyptic content, mingled within the millennial politics. We need to be cautious in assessing this type of material, as it has less clarity of separation between politics, religion and mystical or prophetic inspiration than we find today, when such matters are very carefully compartmentalised and isolated from one another.

The blurring, or perhaps we ought to say resonance, between inspired vision and seeking to instigate political change is particularly strong in two distinct areas of European culture, that of the common man and woman or peasant, and that of the monastic. In the first case this resonance between seeking a better material life free from oppression and seeking a spiritual life holds a vast, intermingled, collective source of pagan and Christian lore, some of it obvious, some of it highly obscure, much of it extremely ancient when traced to its potential roots.

In the second case, that of the monasteries, we have material issuing from centres of learning and spiritual meditation, populated by men and women of all social classes. Active politics played a major role in certain monasteries in Europe.

Prophecies as propaganda have a long history:[18] the art of manipulating opinion through carefully planted 'prophecies' was well known in the Roman Empire, and undoubtedly featured in many cultures long before. But the mass of political prophecies stem from the medieval period onwards, reaching even into the twentieth century when we find constant rumours, if not many factual reports, that printed prophecies were used as propaganda by various nations during the First and Second World Wars.

Sometimes it is difficult to separate the propaganda from actual prophetic work: such is the case of the extremely influential work of Joachim of Fiore.[19] Professor Norman Cohn, in *The Pursuit of the Millennium*, describes Joachim as 'the inventor of a new prophetic system, which was to be the most influential one known to Europe until the appearance of Marxism'. Influential as it certainly was, the Joachite system was not really new, but founded upon perennial traditions. He redefined the concept of Three Worlds and Three

Ages, which corresponded loosely to the concept of the Christian Trinity.

The First Age was that of the Father, and of the Law; the Second Age was of The Son and The Gospel, while the Third Age, yet to come, was to be that of the Holy Spirit. This sequence and its many ramifications were taken literally during and after Joachim's lifetime, when there were a number of upsurges of belief that the Third Age was coming, that the corrupt Church would be overthrown, that Anti-Christ would appear, and that Heaven would descend to Earth.

It is difficult for the modern mind to grasp the fervour of this period, yet we know something of it when we consider the absurdities of New Age enthusiasm today, when many people declare, quite incorrectly, that we are astrologically in the New Age of Aquarius and that all will be well, when in fact, depending on which set of calculation one chooses to apply, the New Age occurs some time well after the year 2,000. Millennial belief, therefore, reoccurs, and has not died away with the death of the Christian religion as a major spiritual and political force.

The Joachite interpretation of Scripture, the Book of Revelation, and other texts, also became fused with a very ancient, deeply rooted collective tradition, that of the sleeping king. This had been applied in Britain to King Arthur, by the Welsh and Bretons to Charlemagne, and was later applied to the Emperor Frederick Barbarossa, the idealised Christian militant ruler, who died of a heart attack while on Crusade.[20] This belief, amplified by various prophetic texts and tales, has its foundation in the pagan sanctity of the king and partner or husband to the Goddess of the Land: we find variants of it until at least as late as the eighteenth century, when people still believed European kings to have the healing touch. Such deeply rooted concepts live on in many forms, and we even find traces of this type of belief applied to the current British heir, Charles, who is outspoken on a number of subjects such as architecture, therapy, and environmental issues.

The Joachite prophecies were attached to Frederick II, grandson of Frederick Barbarossa, giving immediacy to the old dreamlike tales of the sleeping king and coming divinely inspired ruler. He would chastise the wicked Church, he would usher in the New Age, and so forth. When a monk had a vision that, upon his death, Frederick II had descended into Mount Etna, the ancient gateway to the pagan Underworld, it was assumed that Frederick had joined the ranks of the Sleeping Kings, waiting to come again.

The refined spiritual meditations and prophecies of Joachim became the source of a revolutionary fervour and were to inspire many other writers, both sincere and fraudulent, for centuries to follow.

Other prophecies have been written with political ends, and added to the illustrious names of Merlin, Nostradamus, even to the less famous Scottish prophet Thomas Rhymer, who lived in the thirteenth century. As late as the nineteenth century prophecies associated with Thomas were published for popular appeal, while so many items have been added to the names of Merlin and Nostradamus that one must always go to the earliest sources for any accurate or potentially accurate material.

The British Revolutionary movement, which grew out of the dissenting sects, was not without its prophetic fervour, declaring the New Age of spiritual communism. Indeed, communism was born not as Marxism or as a materialist event concurrent with the Russian Revolution, but as a visionary and prophetic movement in seventeenth century England, with obscure sects like the Diggers setting up Heaven on Earth, only to be crushed by the political status quo. Much of the severe suppression of sects such as the Quakers, who were heavily persecuted in Britain, was due to their potentially disruptive prophetic inclinations.

We find prophecy used not only for propaganda, but for satire. The Jacobean comedy *The Birth of Merlin*[21] was revived in the eighteenth century to satirise the British monarchy, as Queen Caroline had imprudently built a folly called Merlin's Cave. The original play was a roaring comedy, but based upon the legends and prophecies of Merlin as originally set out by Geoffrey of Monmouth.

Political and social reforms were inspired by esoteric means in the nineteenth and twentieth centuries, unlikely as this may seem. The Theosophical Society, whom we last mentioned in the context of *flying rolls* (page 17) were very influential in the removal of British rule from India; they also played a vigourous part in the opposition to experiments on animals, a debate that is still active today. The noted reformer and campaigner for women's rights, Annie Besant, was a leading member of the Theosophical Society, taking her guidance from the Hidden Masters, writing prophetically inspired papers, working ceaselessly to change the corrupt culture of the Victorian and Edwardian era. Yet in a recent documentary film dealing in depth with Women's Rights she was omitted, presumably due to her esoteric leanings.

The influential figure of Rudolph Steiner, once a Theosophist, but breaking away to found the Anthroposophical movement, developed a number of effective new techniques in meditation, therapy and education, agriculture, and art. All of his work was founded upon seership. It is rumoured, perhaps not without foundation, that Hitler tried to assassinate Steiner: certainly Steiner's books were banned by the Third Reich.

We hear constant rumours, sometimes breaking into dubious publications, that British Intelligence has a top-secret section employing seers, clairvoyants, and other specialists in esoteric arts. It seems likely that this may indeed have been part of the propaganda machine against the Nazis, who were extremely superstitious, but if most modern clairvoyants are anything to judge by, British Intelligence must be pervaded with ethereal flowers, spirit guides, and messages from defunct great aunts in heavenly gardens.

In recent years fashionable attention has been paid to the prophetic arts of primal people, such as the prophecies of the Hopi Indians. Indeed, prophecy has had a considerable revival in America, where it has always played a role in fundamentalist sects or esoteric cults. Some of this is part of a propaganda machine tying in Christian fundamentalism to the American government. So in a sense the Joachite movement has its latest adherents in the USA, with dogmatic belief in the Book of Revelation, the purging of the world (by nuclear means) and, of course, the saving of the elect.

APPENDIX I
THOMAS RHYMER'S
INITIATION

In the thirteenth century, Thomas of Erceldoune (Earlston), a historical person, became a noted Scottish prophet. His verses dealt entirely with local or Scottish history and made no pretension to international matters. Of value in our present context of a short summary of the elements of prophecy is the means by which he gained his powers of vision. They are described in a traditional ballad, long in oral circulation, and in a Romance text. Thomas is also said to be the author of the first known text of Tristan, though this is doubtful.[22]

The experience of Thomas is a classic visitation to the Underworld, a mysterious realm, of major importance in both Celtic and classical traditions. In ancient Greece and Rome the shades of the dead were summoned from the Underworld for oracular purposes, sometimes profound, sometimes of the most trivial nature.[23] In the Celtic tradition the Underworld was identified with the *sidh* of the realm of Fairy, ruled over by a terrible and beautiful Queen. We may briefly summarise the initiatory experience of Thomas, as described in various texts:

1. The poet sits under a hawthorn tree.
2. In repose he is visited by a beautiful woman riding upon a powerful horse with silver bells upon its bridle.
3. He courts her, and she demands that he ride away with her. He says that she must be the Queen of Heaven, but she declares that

she is the Queen of Elfland or Fairyland.

4 The steed flies faster than the wind, and they travel into a dimension under the ground. He is carried physically into this realm.

5. In this Underworld there is no sunlight or moonlight, but starlight only.

6. A roaring sea is heard, and the horse wades through a river of blood.

7. Eventually they come to a wondrous tree in the Underworld, and Thomas offers to pick its fruit for the woman.

8. She refuses his offer, and says that if he touches the fruit it will drive him mad or kill him.

9. She offers him instead bread and wine, and then says that she will show him three wonders.

10. The wonders are three roads, the thorny road of righteousness, the wide road of wickedness, and the winding road to Elfland, where they must travel.

11. He stays in that place for seven years as her servant, and when he emerges has the gift of prophecy. Sometimes he has other gifts also, such as a harp, or magical cloak.

This is a poetical reworking of an initiatory technique, and it is interesting to find it preserved in ballad form as late as the nineteenth century. A modern descendant of Thomas the Rhymer, who was also known as Lord Learmont, is Michael Learmontov, the Russian poet, so the poetic force still runs on. If we condense the sequence even further, we find some of the basic keys to prophetic inspiration:

1. The would-be seer must attune to the land.

2. He must visualise or invoke the Goddess of the Land.

3. He passes in visualisation into the Underworld.

4. He experiences the genetic or ancestral consciousness which is inherent in the blood.

5. He has a vision of the Tree of Life at the centre of the Underworld, which being lit by stars only, is also the centre of the universe.

6. He offers to pick the fruit of this tree even if it means madness or death.

7. The Queen or Goddess protects him from insanity by giving him the fruit in an acceptable form – bread and wine. There are echoes of the various transubstantiation rites in this sequence.

8. He then sees a further vision of three roads representing the spiritual choices of humanity: his road is the one to Elfland, Fairyland, the home of the Queen.
9. He serves the Queen for seven years, and emerges with prophetic gifts. We might take this to mean that his training or period of psychic transformation is extensive.

APPENDIX II
RUDOLPH STEINER AND ANCESTRAL CONSCIOUSNESS

Rudolph Steiner describes the collective awareness that plays an important role in some traditions of prophecy, though not in all, in the following way (from *The Occult Significance of the Blood*, New York, 1907):

Ancestry, or descent, places us where we stand in accordance with the law of blood-relationship. A person is born of a connection, a race, a tribe, a line of ancestors, and what these ancestors have bequeathed to him is expressed in his blood. In the blood is gathered together, as it were, all the material past has constructed in man; and in the blood is also being formed all that is being prepared for the future.

When, therefore, man temporarily suppresses his higher consciousness, when he is in a hypnotic state, or one of somnambulism, or when he is atavistically clairvoyant, then he descends to a far deeper consciousness, one wherein he becomes dreamily cognizant of the great cosmic laws, but nevertheless perceives them much more clearly than the most vivid dreams of ordinary sleep. At such times the activity of his brain is in abeyance, and during states of the deepest somnambulism this applies also to the spinal cord. The man experiences the activities of his sympathetic nervous system; that is to say, in a dim and hazy fashion he senses the life of the entire cosmos. At such times the blood no longer expresses pictures of the inner life which are produced by means of the brain, but it presents those which the outer world has formed in it. Now, however, we must bear in mind that the forces of his ancestors have helped to make him what he is. Just as he inherits the shape of his nose from an ancestor, so does he inherit the form of his whole body. At such times of suppressed consciousness he sense his ancestors within him, even as during his waking consciousness he sense the pictures of the outer world; that is to say, his forbears are active in his blood, and at such a time he dimly takes part in their remote life.

Everything in the world is in a state of evolution, human consciousness included. Man has not always had the consciousness he now possesses; when we go back to the times of our earliest ancestors, we find a consciousness of a very different kind. At the present time man in his waking-life perceives external things through the agency of his sense and forms ideas about them. These ideas about the external world work on his blood. Everything, therefore, of which he has been the recipient as the result of sense-experience, lives and is active in his blood; his memory is stored with these experiences of his senses. Yet, on the other hand, the man of to-day is no longer conscious of what he possesses in his inward bodily life by inheritance from his ancestors. He knows naught concerning the forms of his inner organs; but in earlier times this was otherwise. There then lived within the blood not only what the senses had received from the external world, but also that which is contained within the bodily form; and as that bodily form was inherited from his ancestors, man sensed their life within himself.

If we think of a heightened form of this consciousness, we shall have some idea of how this was also expressed in a corresponding form of memory. A person experiencing no more than what he perceives by his senses, remembers no more than the events connected with those outward sense-experiences. He can only be aware of such things as he may have experienced in this way since his childhood. But with prehistoric man the case was different. Such a man sensed what was within him, and as this inner experience was the result of heredity, he passed through the experiences of his ancestors by means of his inner faculty. He remembered not only his own childhood, but also the experiences of his ancestors. This life of his ancestors was, in fact, ever present in the pictures which his blood received, for, incredible as it may seem to the materialistic ideas of the present day, there was at one time a form of consciousness by means of which men considered not only their own sense-perceptions as their own experiences, but also the experiences of their forefathers. In those times, when they said, 'I have experienced such and such a thing,' they alluded not only to what had happened to themselves personally, but also to the experiences of their ancestors, for they could remember them.

This earlier consciousness was, it is true, of a very dim kind, very hazy as compared to man's waking consciousness at the present day. It partook more of the nature of a vivid dream, but, on the other hand, it embraced far more than does our present consciousness. The son felt himself connected with his father and his grandfather as one 'I,' because he felt their experiences as if they were his own. And because man was possessed of this consciousness, because he lived not only in his own personal world but because within him there dwelt also the consciousness of preceding generations, in naming himself he included in that name all belonging to his ancestral line. Father, son, grandson, etc., designated by one name that which was common to them all, that which passed through them all; in short, a person felt himself to be merely a member of an entire line of descendants. This sensation was a true and actual one.

APPENDIX III
NOSTRADAMUS' PROPHETIC EPISTLE TO HENRY II OF FRANCE

There are many translations and interpretation of the *Centuries* currently available, but popular editions usually exclude the important *Preface* (quoted in full in Chapter 7), and the prophetic *Epistle*, quoted below. This text should be compared in terms of the imagery to that of Merlin, and to the extracts from Biblical prophecies quoted in our other chapters.

EPISTLE TO HENRY II

To the most invincible, very puissant, and most Christian Henry King of France the Second: Michael Nostradamus, his most humble, most obedient servant and subject, wishes victory and happiness.

For that sovereign observation that I had, O most Christian and very victorious King, since that my face, long obscured with cloud, presented itself before the deity of your measureless Majesty, since that in that I have been perpetually dazzled, never failing to honour and worthily revere that day, when first before it, as before a singularly humane majesty, I presented myself. I searched for some occasion by which to manifest good heart and frank courage, by the means of which I might grow into greater knowledge of your serene Majesty. I soon found in effect it was impossible for me to declare it, considering the contrast of the solitariness of my long obnubilation and obscurity, and my being suddenly thrust into brilliancy, and transported into the presence of the sovereign eye of the first monarch of the universe. Likewise I have long hung in doubt as to whom I ought to dedicate these three Centuries to, the remainder of my Prophecies amounting now to a thousand. I have long meditated on an act of such audacity. I have at last ventured to address your Majesty, and was not daunted from it as Plutarch, that grave author, relates in the life of Lycurgus, that, seeing the gifts and presents that were made in the way of sacrifice at the temples of the immortal gods in that age, many were staggered at the expense, and dared not approach the temple to present anything.

Notwithstanding this, I saw your royal splendour to be accompanied with an incomparable humanity, and paid my addresses to it, not as to those Kings of Persia whom it was not permissible to approach. But to a very prudent and very wise Prince I have dedicated my nocturnal and prophetic calculations, composed out of a natural instinct, and accompanied by a poetic fervour, rather than according to the strict rules of poetry. Most part, indeed, has been composed and adjusted by astronomical calculation corresponding to the years, months, and weeks, of the regions, countries, and for the most part town and cities, throughout Europe, Africa, and a part of Asia, which nearest approach each other in all these climates, and this is composed in a natural manner. Possibly some may answer – who, if so, had better blow his nose [that he may see the clearer by it] – that the rhythm is as easy to be understood, as the sense is hard to get at. Therefore, O most gracious King, the bulk of the prophetic quatrains are so rude, that there is no making way through them, nor is there any interpreter of them. Nevertheless, being always anxious to set down the years, towns, and regions cited, where the events are to occur, even from the year 1585, and the year 1606, dating from the present time, which is the 14th of March, 1557.

Then passing far beyond to things which shall happen at the commencement of the seventh millenary, deeply calculated, so far as my astronomic calculus, and other knowledge, has been able to reach, to the time when the adversaries of Jesus Christ and of His Church shall begin to multiply in great force. The whole has been composed and calculated on days and hours of best election and disposition, and with all the accuracy I could attain to. At a moment 'Minerva libera et non invita,' ['When

Minerva was free and favourable,'] my calculations looking forward to events through a space of time to come that nearly equals that of the past even up to the present, and by this they will know in the lapse of time and in all regions what is to happen, all written down thus particularly, immingled with nothing superfluous.

Notwithstanding that some say, 'Quod de futuris non est determinata omnino veritas,' ['There can be no truth entirely determined for certain which concerns the future.'] I will confess, Sire, that I believed myself capable of presage from the natural instinct I inherit of my ancestors, adjusted and regulated by elaborate calculation, and the endeavour to free the soul, mind, and heart from all care, solicitude, and anxiety, by resting and tranquilizing the spirit, which finally has all to be completed and perfected in one respect tripode æneo, by the brazen tripod. With all this there will be many to attribute to me as mine, things no more mine than nothing. The Almighty alone, who strictly searches the human heart, pious, just, and pitiful, is the true Judge; to Him I pray to defend me from the calumny of wicked men. Such persons, with equal calumny, will bring into question how all your ancient progenitors the Kings of France have cured the evil; how those of other nations have cured the bite of serpents; others have had a certain instinct in the art of divination, and other faculties that would be too long to recount here. Notwithstanding such as cannot be restrained from the exercise of the malignancy of the evil spirit, by the lapse of time, and after my extinction here on earth, my writings will be more valued than during my lifetime.

However, if I err in calculation of ages, or find myself unable to please all the world, may it please your Imperial Majesty to forgive me, for I protest before God and His saints, that I purpose to insert nothing whatever in writing this present Epistle that shall militate against the true Catholic Faith, while consulting the astronomical calculations to the very best of my knowledge. For the stretch of time of our forefathers which has gone before is such, submitting myself to the direction of the soundest chronologists, that the first man, Adam, was about one thousand two hundred and forty years before Noah, not computing time by Gentile records, such as Varro has committed to writing, but taking simply the Sacred Scriptures for the guide in my astronomic reckonings, to the best of my feeble understanding. After Noah, from him and the universal deluge, about one thousand and fourscore years, came Abraham, who was a sovereign astrologer according to some; he first invented the Chaldæan alphabet. Then came Moses, about five hundred and fifteen or sixteen years later. Between the time of David and Moses five hundred and seventy years elapsed. Then after the time of David and the time of our Saviour and Redeemer, Jesus Christ, born of a pure Virgin, there elapsed (according to some chronographers) one thousand three hundred and fifty years.

Some, indeed, may object to this supputation as not true, because it varies from that of Eusebius. Since the time of the human redemption to the hateful apostacy of the Saracens there have been six hundred and twenty-one years, or thereabouts. Now, from this it is easy to gather what time has elapsed if my supputation be not good and available for all nations, for that all is calculated by the celestial courses, associated in my case with an emotion that steals over me at certain subsecival hours from an emotional tendency handed down to me from a line of ancestors. But the injuriousness of our time, O most serene Sovereign, requires that such secret events should not transpire, except in enigmatic sentences, having but one sense and one only meaning, and quite unmingled with calculation that is of ambiguity or amphibology. Say, rather, under a veiled obscurity from some natural emotional effusion, that resembles the sentential delivery of the thousand and two Prophets, that have been from the Creation of the world, according to the calculation and Punic *Chronicle of Joel: 'Effundum spiritum meum super omnem carnem, et prophetabunt filii vestri, et filæ vestræ.'* See Joel ii.28. But this prophecy proceeded from the mouth of the Holy Spirit, which was the sovereign power eternal, in conjunction with the celestial bodies, has caused some of the number to predict great and marvellous events.

As to myself in this place, I set up no claim to such a title – never, please God. I fully confess that all proceeds from God, and for that I return Him thanks, honour, and immortal praise, and have mingled nothing with it of the divination which proceeds *à fato*, but *à Deo, à naturâ*, and for the most part accompanied with the movement of the celestial courses. Much as, if looking into a burning mirror [we see], as with darkened vision, the great events, sad or portentous, and calamitous occurrences that are about to fall upon the principal worshippers. First upon the temples of God, secondly upon such as have their support from the earth,

119

this decadence draweth nigh, with a thousand other calamitous incidents that in the course of time will be known to happen.

For God will take notice of the long barrenness of the great Dame, who afterwards will conceive two principal children. But, she being in great danger, the girl she will give birth to with risk at her age of death in the eighteenth year, and not possible to outlive the thirty-sixth, will leave three males and one female, and he will have two who never had any of the same father. The three brothers will be so different, though united and agreed, that the three and four parts of Europe will tremble. By the youngest in years will the Christian monarchy be sustained and augmented; heresies spring up and suddenly cast down, the Arabs driven back, kingdoms united, and new laws promulgated. Of the other children the first shall possess the furious crowned Lions, holding their paws upon the bold escutcheon. The second, accompanied by the Latins, shall penetrate so far that a second trembling and furious descent shall be made, descending Mons Jovis to mount the Pyrenees, shall not be translated to the antique monarchy, and a third inundation of human blood shall arise and March for a long while will not be found in Lent. The daughter shall be given for the preservation of the Christian Church, the dominator falling into the Pagan sect of new infidels, and she will have two children, the one fidelity, the other infidelity, by the confirmation of the Catholic Church. The other, who to his great confusion and tardy repentance wished to ruin her, will have three regions over a wide extent of leagues, that is to say, Roumania, Germany, and Spain, which will entail great intricacy of military handling, stretching from the 50th to the 52nd degree of latitude. And they will have to respect the more distant religions of Europe and the north above the 48th degree of latitude, which at first in a vain timidity will tremble, and then the more western, southern, and eastern will tremble. Their power will become such, that what is brought about by union and concord will prove insuperable by warlike conquest. By nature they will be equal, but exceedingly different in faith.

After this the sterile Dame, of greater power than the second, shall be received by two nations, by the first made obstinate by him who had power over all, by the second, and third, that shall extend his forces towards the circuit of the east of Europe; [arrived] there his standards will stop and succumb, but by sea he will run on to Trinacria and the Adriatic with his myrmidons. The Germans will succumb wholly and the Barbaric sect will be disquieted and driven back by the whole of the Latin race. Then shall begin the grand Empire of Antichrist in the Atila and Xerxes, to descend with innumerable multitudes, so that the coming of the Holy Spirit, issuing from the 48th degree, shall make a transmigration, chasing away the abomination of Antichrist, that made war upon the royal person of the great vicar of Jesus Christ, and against His Church, and reign *per tempus, et in occasione temporis* [for a time, and to the end of time]. This will be preceded by an eclipse of the sun, more obscure and tenebrose than has ever been since the creation of the world, up to the death and passion of Jesus Christ, and from thence till now. There will be in the month of October a grand revolution made, such that one would think that the librating body of the earth had lost its natural movement in the abyss of perpetual darkness. There will be seen precursive signs in the spring-time, and after extreme changes ensuing, reversal of kingdoms, and great earthquakes. All this accompanied with the procreations of the New Babylon, a miserable prostitute big with the abomination of the first holocaust. It will continue for only seventy-three years seven months.

Then there will issue from the stock so long time barren, proceeding from the 50th degree, one who will renovate the whole Christian Church. A great peace, union, and concord will then spring up between some of the children of races opposed to each other and separated by diverse kingdoms. Such a peace shall be set up, that the instigator and promoter of military faction by means of the diversity of religions, shall dwell attached to the bottom of the abyss, and united to the kingdom of the furious, who shall counterfeit the wise. The countries, towns, cities, and provinces that had forsaken their old customs to free themselves, enthralling themselves more deeply, shall become secretly weary of their liberty, and, true religion lost, shall commence by striking off to the left, to return more than ever to the right.

Then replacing holiness, so long desecrated by their former writings, afterwards the result will be that the great dog will issue as an irresistible mastiff who will destroy everything, even to all that may have been prepared in time past, till the churches will be restored as at first, and the clergy reinstated in their pristine condition; till it lapses again into whoredom and luxury, to commit and perpetrate a thousand crimes. And, drawing near to another desolation, then, when she shall be at her highest and sublimest point of dignity, the kings and generals will come up, and her two swords will be taken from her, and nothing will be left her but the semblance of them. From which by the means of the crookedness that draweth them, the people causing it to go straight, and not willing to submit unto them by the end opposite to the sharp hand that toucheth the ground they shall provoke. Until there shall be born unto the branch a long time sterile, one who shall deliver the French people from the benign slavery that they voluntarily submitted to, putting himself under the protection of Mars, and stripping Jupiter of all his honours and dignities, for the city constituted free and seated in another narrow Mesopotamia. The chief and governor shall be cast from the midst, and set in a place of the air, ignorant of the conspiracy of the conspirators with the second Thrasibulus, who for a long time had prepared all this. Then shall the impurities and abominations be with great shame set forth and manifested to the darkness of the veiled light, shall cease towards the end of his reign, and the chiefs of the Church shall evince but little of the love of God, whilst many of them shall apostatize from the true faith.

Of the three sects (Lutheran, Catholic, and Mahometan), that which is in the middle, by the action of its own worshippers, will be thrown a little into decadence. The first totally throughout Europe, and the chief part of Africa exterminated by the third, by means of the poor in spirit, who by the madness engendered of libidinous luxury, will commit adultery. The people will pull down the pillar, and chase away the adherents of the legislators, and it shall seem, from the kingdoms weakened by the Orientals, that God the Creator has loosed Satan from the infernal prisons, to make room for the great Dog and Dohan, which will make so great and injurious a breach in the Churches, that neither the reds nor the whites, who are without eyes and without hands, cannot judge of the situation, and their power will be taken from them. Then shall commence a persecution of the Church such as never was before. While this is enacting, such a pestilence shall spring up that out of three parts of mankind two shall be removed. To such a length will this proceed that one will neither know nor recognize the fields or houses, and grass will grow in the streets of the cities as high as a man's knees. To the clergy there shall be a total desolation, and the martial men shall usurp what shall come back from the City of the Sun, and from Malta, and the Islands of Hières, and the great chain of the port shall be opened that takes its name from the marine ox.

A new incursion shall be made from the maritime shores, eager to give the leap of liberty since the first taking by the Mahometans. Their assaults shall not be at all in vain, and in the place where the habitation of Abraham was, it shall be assailed by those who hold the Jovialists in reverence. The city of Achem (in the Island of Sumatra) shall be encompassed and assaulted on all sides by a great force of armed men. Their maritime forces shall be weakened by the Westerns. Upon this kingdom a great desolation shall come, and the great cities shall be depopulated, and such as enter in shall come under the vengeance of the wrath of God. The Holy Sepulchre, for so long a period an object of great veneration, shall remain exposed to the blighting dew of evening under the stars of heaven, and of the sun and moon. The holy place shall be converted into a stable for cattle small and large, applied to other base purposes. Oh, what a calamitous time will that be for women with child! for then the Sultan of the East will be vanquished, driven for the most part by the Northern and Western men, who will kill him, overthrow him, and put the rest to flight, and his children, the offspring of many women, imprisoned. Then will come to its fulfilment the prophecy of the Royal Prophet, 'Ut audiret gemitus compeditorum, et solveret filios interemptorum.' ('Let the sighing of the prisoner come before thee, to release the children of death') (Ps. 1xxviii. 11).

What great oppression shall then fall upon the princes and rulers of kingdoms, even on those who are maritime and Oriental, their tongues intermingled from all nations of the earth! Tongues of the Latin nations, mingled with Arabic and North-African communication. All the Eastern kings will be driven away, overthrown, and exterminated, not at all by means of the kings of the North and the drawing near of our age, but by means of the three secretly united who seek out death and snares by ambush sprung upon one another. The renewal of this Triumvirate shall endure for seven years, while its renown shall spread all over the world, and the sacrifice of the holy and immaculate wafer shall be upheld. Then shall two lords of the North conquer the Orientals, and so great report and tumultuary warfare shall issue from these that all the East shall tremble at the noise of these two brothers of the North, who are yet not brothers. And because, Sire, by this discourse I almost introduce confusion into these predictions as to the time when the event of each shall fall out; for the detailed account of the time that follows is very little conformable, if at all, to what I gave above, that indeed could not err, being by astronomic rule and consonant with the Holy Scriptures themselves.

Had I wished to give to every quatrain its detailed date, it could easily have been done, but it would not have been agreeable to all, and still less to interpret them, Sire, until your Majesty should have fully sanctioned me to do this, in order not to furnish calumniators with an opportunity to injure me. Always reckoning the years since the creation of the world to the birth of Noah as being 1506 years, and from that to the completion of the building of the ark at the period of the universal deluge 600 years elapsed (let them be solar years, or lunar, or mixed), I hold that the Scripture takes them to be solar. At the conclusion of this 600 years, Noah entered the ark to escape the deluge. The deluge was universal over the earth, and lasted one year and two months. From the conclusion of the deluge to the birth of Abraham there elapsed 295 years, and 100 years from that to the birth of Isaac. From Isaac to Jacob 60 years. From the time he went into Egypt until his coming out of it was 130 years; and from the entry of Jacob into Egypt to his exit was 430 years; and from that to the building of the Temple by Solomon in the fortieth year of his reign, makes 480 years. From the building of the Temple to Jesus Christ, according to the supputation of the Hierographs, there passed 490 years. Thus by this calculation that I have made, collecting it out of the sacred writings, there are about 4173 years and eight months less or more. Now, from Jesus Christ, in that there is such a diversity of opinion, I pass it by, and having calculated the present prophecies in accordance with the order of the chain which contains the revolution, and the whole by astronomical rule, together with my own hereditary instinct. After some time, and including in it the period Saturn takes to turn between the 7th of April up to the 25th of August; Jupiter from the 14th of June to the 7th of October; Mars from the 17th of April to the 22nd of June; Venus from the 9th of April to the 22nd of May; Mercury from the 3rd of February to the 24th of the same; afterwards from the 1st of June to the 24th of the same; and from the 25th of September to the 16th of October, Saturn in Capricorn, Jupiter in Aquarius, Mars in Scorpio, Venus in Pisces, Mercury within a month in Capricorn, Aquarius, and Pisces; the moon in Aquarius, the Dragon's head in Libra, the tail in her sign opposite. Following the conjunction of Jupiter to Mercury, with a quadrin aspect of Mars to Mercury, and the head of the Dragon shall be with a conjunction of Sol with Jupiter, the year shall be peaceful without eclipse.

Then will be the commencement (of a period) that will comprehend in itself what will long endure [i.e. the vulgar advent of the French Revolution], and in its first year there shall be a great persecution of the Christian Church, fiercer than that in Africa, and this will burst out the year one thousand seven hundred and ninety-two; they will think it to be a renovation of time. After this the people of Rome will begin to reconstitute themselves, and to chase away the obscurity of darkness, recovering some share of their ancient brightness, but not without much division and continual changes. Venice after that, in great force and power, shall raise her wings very high, not much short of the force of ancient Rome. At that time great Byzantine sails, associated with the Piedmontese by the help and power of the North, will so restrain them that the two Cretans will not be able to maintain their faith. The arks built by the ancient warriors will accompany them to the waves of Neptune. In the Adriatic there will be such permutations, that what was united will be separated, and that will be reduced to a house which before was a great city, including the Pampotan and Mesopotamia of Europe, to 45, and others to 41, 42, and 47. And in that time and those countries the infernal power will set the power of the adversaries of its law against the Church of Jesus Christ. This will constitute the second Antichrist, which will persecute that Church and its true vicar, by means of the power of the temporal kings, who in their ignorance will be reduced by tongues that will cut more than any sword in the hands of a madman.

The said reign of Antichrist will last only to the death of him who was born near the [commencement] of the century, and of the other in the city of Plancus, accompanied by him the elect of Modena, Fulcy by Ferara, upheld by the Adriatic Piedmontese, and the proximity of the great Trinacria. Afterwards the Gallic Ogmion shall pass the Mount Jovis, accompanied by so great a number that from afar the Empire shall be presented with its grand law, and then and for some time after shall be profusely shed the blood of the innocent by the guilty recently elevated to power. Then by great deluges the memory of things contained in such instruments shall suffer incalculable loss, even to the Alphabet itself. This will happen among the Northerns. By the Divine Will once again Satan will be bound, and universal peace established amongst mankind, and the Church of Jesus Christ delivered from all tribulation, although the Azostains would desire to mix with the honey the gall of their pestilent seduction. This will be near the seventh millenary, when the sanctuary of Jesus Christ will no longer be trodden down by the infidels who come from the North; the world approaching its great conflagration, although by my supputation in my prophecies, the course of time runs much farther on.

In the epistle that some years since I dedicated to my son Cæsar Nostradamus, I have openly enough declared some points without presage. But here, Sire, are comprised many great and marvellous events to come, which those who follow after us shall see. And during the said astrological supputation, harmonized with the sacred Scriptures, the persecution of the Ecclesiastics shall take its rise in the power of the kings of the North, united with the Easterns. And this persecution shall last eleven years, or somewhat less, by which time the chief Northern king shall pass away, which years being run, a united Southern king shall succeed, which shall still more fiercely persecute the clergy of the Church for the space of three years by the Apostolical seduction of one who will take away all the absolute power from the Church Militant, and holy people of God who observe its ritual, and the whole order of religion shall be greatly persecuted and so afflicted that the blood of true ecclesiastics shall float everywhere. To one of those horrible temporal kings such praise shall be given by his adherents that he will have shed more human blood of innocent ecclesiastics, than any could do of wine. This king will commit crimes against the Church that are incredible. Human blood will flow in the public streets and churches, like water after impetuous rain, and will crimson with blood the neighbouring rivers, and by another naval war redden the sea to such a degree that one king shall say to another, 'Bellis rubuit navalibus æquor.' ['The sea blushed red with the blood of naval fights.'] Then in the same year and those following there will ensue the most horrible pestilence and the most astonishing on account of the famine that will precede, and such tribulation that nothing approaching it ever happened since the first foundation of the Christian Church; this also throughout all the Latin regions, leaving traces in all the countries under the rule of Spain.

Then the third King of the North, hearing the complaint of the people from his principal title, will raise up a mighty army, and pass through the limits of his last progenitors and great-grandfathers, to him who will replace almost everything in its old condition. The great Vicar of the Cope shall be put back to his pristine state; but, desolated and abandoned by all, will return to the sanctuary destroyed by Paganism, when the Old and New Testament will be thrust out and burnt. After that Antichrist will be the infernal prince. Then at this last epoch, all the kingdoms of Christianity, as well as of the infidel world, will be shaken during the space of twenty-five years, and the wars and battles will be more grievous, and the towns, cities, castles, and all other edifices will be burnt, desolated, and destroyed with much effusion of vestal blood, married women and widows violated, sucking children dashed and broken against the walls of towns; and so many evils will be committed by means of Satan, the prince infernal, that nearly all the world will become undone and desolated. Before the events occur certain strange birds will cry in the air, 'To-day! to-day!' and after a given time will disappear. After this has endured for a certain length of time, there will be almost renewed another reign of Saturn, the age of gold. God the Creator shall say, hearing the affliction of His people, Satan shall be precipitated and bound in the bottomless abyss, and then shall commence between God and men a universal peace. There he shall abide for the space of a thousand years, and shall turn his greatest force against the power of the Church, and shall then be bound again.

How justly are all these figures adapted by the divine letters to visible celestial things, that is to say, by Saturn, Jupiter, and Mars, and others in conjuction with them, as may be seen more at large by some of the quatrains! I would have calculated it more deeply, and adapted the one to the other; but, seeing, O most serene King, that some who are given to censure will raise a difficulty, I shall take the opportunity to retire my pen and seek my nocturnal repose. '*Multa etiam, O Rex potentissime præclara, et sane in brevi ventura, sed omnia in hâc tuâ Epistola, innectere non possumus, nec volumus, sed ad intellegenda quædam facta, horrida fata pauca libanda sunt, quamvis tanta sit in omnes tua amplitudo et humanitas homines, deosque pietas, ut solos amplissimo et Christianissimo Regis nomine, et ad quem summa totius religionis auctoritas deferatur dignus esse videare.*' ['Many things, O most potent king of all, of the most remarkable kind are shortly to happen, that I neither could nor would interweave them all into this epistle; but in order to comprehend certain facts, a few horrible destinies must be set down in extract, although your amplitude and humanity towards all men is so great, and your piety to the gods, that you alone seem worthy of the grand title of the most Christian King, and to whom the highest authority in all religion should be deferred.'] But I shall only beseech you, O most clement King, by this your singular and most prudent goodness, to understand rather the desire of my heart, and the sovereign wish I have to obey your most excellent Majesty, ever since my eyes approached so nearly to your solar splendour, than the grandeur of my work can attain to or acquire.

Faciebat MICHAEL NOSTRADRAMUS
Solonœ Petræ Provinciæ.

From Salon this 27th June, 1558.

NOTES

1. Stewart, R. J., *The Prophetic Vision of Merlin* and *The Mystic Life of Merlin*, (Penguin Arkana, Harmondsworth, 1986 and 1989). Contain translations of the prophecies and the biography of Merlin from the works of Geoffrey of Monmouth (12th c.) with detailed commentaries and comparisons.
2. Stewart, R. J., *Elements of Creation Myth* (Element, Shaftesbury, 1989).
3. Dunne, J. W., *An Experiment with Time* (Faber, London, 1939).
4. Stewart R. J., *Music and the Elemental Psyche* (Aquarian Press, Wellingborough, 1987). Also Stewart, *Music, Power, Harmony* (Blandford Press, London, 1990).
5. Stewart, R. J., *The Merlin Tarot* (Aquarian Press, Wellingborough, 1988). Book and full colour deck of cards (illustrated by Miranda Gray). Covers many aspects of symbolism, visualisation, prediction, and modes of consciousness. Stewart, *Advanced Merlin Tarot*, Vol. II, (forthcoming, 1991).
6. Sheldrake, R., *The Presence of the Past* (Collins, London, 1988). Sheldrake, *A New Science of Life* (Blond, London, 1985).
7. Ross, A., *The Folklore of the Scottish Highlands* (Batsford, London, 1976). Martin, M., *A Description of the Western Islands of Scotland* (1703, repr. 1934). Also Stewart, R. J., *Robert Kirk, Walker between Worlds* (Element Books, Shaftesbury, 1990). Stewart, R. J., *Cuchullainn* (Firebird Books, Poole, 1988).
8. See note 5.

9. See note 1.
10. See note 5.
11. Allen, R. H., *Star Names, Their Lore and Meaning* (New York). Lum, P., *The Stars in Our Heavens* (London).
12. Stewart, R. J., *The Underworld Initiation* (Aquarian Press, Wellingborough, 1985 and 1988). Stewart, R. J. and Matthews, J., *Legendary Britain* (Blandford Press, London, 1989). *The Waters of the Gap* (Ashgrove Press, Bath, 1989).
13. Matthews, J., 'Merlin's Esplumoir' in R. J. Stewart (ed.), *Merlin and Woman* (Blandford Press, 1988).
14. Stewart, R. J., *Living Magical Arts* (Blandford Press, Poole and London, 1987 and 1988). Stewart, *Advanced Magical Arts* (Element Books,Shaftesbury, 1988).
15. Chadwick, N. K., *The Colonization of Brittany from Celtic Britain*, Proceedings of the British Academy, Vol. II (Oxford University Press, London 1965).
16. Stewart, R. J. (ed.), *The Book of Merlin*, various contributors (Blandford Press, 1987 and 1988).
17. See note 1.
18. Taylor, R. T., *The Political Prophecy in England* (Columbia University Press, 1911).
19. Cohn, N., *The Pursuit of the Millennium* (Paladin, London, 1984). Reeves, M., *Joachim of Fiore and the Prophetic Future* (SPCK, London, 1976).
20. Stewart, R. J., *Barbarossa* (Firebird Books, Poole, 1988).
21. Stewart, R. J. (ed.), *The Birth of Merlin or The Childe Hath Found his Father*, new edn with additional chapters by Denise Coffey and Roy Hudd, Foreword by Professor Harold Brooks (Element Books, Shaftesbury, 1989).
22. See note 12.
23. Luck, G., *Arcana Mundi, Magic and the Occult in the Greek and Roman Worlds* (Crucible, Wellingborough, 1987). Cumont, F., *Oriental Religions in Roman Paganism* (Dover, New York, 1956).

FURTHER
READING

Bevan, E., *Sibyls and Seers. A Survey of Some Ancient Theories of Revelation and Inspiration* (George Allen & Unwin, London, 1928).

Burnham, J. M., 'A Study of Thomas of Erceldoune,'
Publications of the Modern Language Association, vol. xxiii (1908).

Campbell, J. G., *Witchcraft and Second Sight in the Highlands and Islands of Scotland* (Glasgow, 1902).

Cheetham, E., *The Prophecies of Nostradamus* (Corgi, London, 1981).

Heywood, T., *The Life of Merlin with his Strange Prophecies: a Chronographical History* (London, 1641; repr. Carmarthen, 1812, and Jones (Wales), Pwllheli 1987).

Smith, C. F., *John Dee* (Constable, London, 1909).

INDEX